MW00909561

Historic Landmarks of
LAHORE
An Account of Protected Monuments

Ihsan H. Nadiem

954.9143 Ihsan H. Nadiem
     Historic Landmarks of Lahore: An
Account of Protected Monuments / Ihsan H.
Nadiem. -Lahore: Sang-e-Meel
Publications, 2006.
     184pp. : Photos
     1. History - Lahore. 2. Pakistan -
History. I. Title.

2006
Published by:
Niaz Ahmad
Sang-e-Meel Publications,
Lahore.

Designed & Printed by:

Topical Printers

Photography: Ihsan H. Nadiem

ISBN 969-35-1869-1

SANG-E-MEEL PUBLICATIONS
Chowk Urdu Bazar Lahore. Pakistan. Phone 7667970
Phones: 7220100 - 7228143 - 7667970 Fax: 7245101
http://www. ang-e-meel.com e-mail: smp@sang-e-meel.com
25-Shahrah-e-Pakistan (Lower Mall), P.O. Box 997 Lahore-54000 Pakistan

To

Muhammad Rafique Dogar,

In appreciation of his personal efforts in serving
the cause of Historic Landmarks of Lahore.

Contents

Explanations:

Preface

Lahore, with its natural location at the ancient routes connecting the West and the Central Asia with the heart of South Asia Subcontinent, has been the rendezvous of many an adventurer, who came storming with swooping armies and their followers – some of them even settling here afterwards. During the age of the empires that had subjugated most of the Subcontinent with their headquarters around Delhi, it hosted for quite durations the royalty and their entourages on way to or from Kashmir and Kabul. No wonder then it was a sort of second home to them all. The city and its environs were thus able to earn a vast wealth of physical legacy spread over a broad canvas of time. This corporal heritage later enticed the historians, scholars and other chroniclers to write on it with the result that there is quite a treasure in literature on this subject.

However, almost all of these narrations of its antiquity are more of academic nature and hardly bring them closer to the discerning reader. They usually describe their physical features and extol the beauty in them and scarcely bring home the down-to-earth facts about their state of preservation or their plight in the present age of altogether changed set of human values in our society. This treatise aims at making a permanent record of the architectural heritage, which had been valued as landmarks at official level and thus protected under the meanings of the relevant law. It seemed all the more necessary that quite a few among them are getting obliterated or so heavily encroached upon that their continued survival is threatened by the very people, who should have been proud of their legacy and guarded them most jealously. The ignorance – or lukewarm attitude – of the general public towards this highly prized heritage is, of course, lamentable but what is more shocking and disturbing is the stance of the officials adopted through omission or commission. Under these circumstances of pathetic visions this treatise aims at arousing – to whatever degree it can

– the consciousness of all concerned to a place of reverence and importance of these landmarks. The other target it endeavours at is to record their data and to publish in a volume to give it a lasting value, so as to reach a larger segment of readers. It seemed very necessary in view of the present unenviable state of record-keeping, which would make their authentic documentation even in foreseeable future almost inaccessible to scholars and general public alike.

This treatise is divided into three chapters: the first one introduces Lahore and gives in passing the history of awareness of the importance of the Heritage – or antiquity – in the broader perspective of the South Asia Subcontinent while also dilating at the relatively glaring examples of the mistreatment of prized monuments in this city; in the second part the whole record of the legacy protected under the relevant law hence recognizing its importance, has been given. In this chapter information found in the official records has heavily been relied upon though in no way it is just a compilation of the available record as it deals with the subject on the basis of the fresh study. The last portion reproduces, as Annexures, some records, which seem necessary in having better understanding of the attitude of the official agencies charged with the responsibility of safeguarding the priceless inheritance of not only the Pakistani nation but also the whole world at large. This may help in guiding people in authority to evaluate and assess the environment of their relevant agencies and the ways they adopt to beat the positive requirements of preserving, maintaining and administering the treasures from the past under their charge.

It may be mentioned here that the Landmarks included in this treatise are only those, which have been notified as protected by the Federal Government. Although the Antiquities Act of 1975 defines the word 'ancient' for the purpose of law as "an antiquity which has been in existence for a period of not less than seventy five years" yet a cursory look at the relevant list would tell that, except for a few National Monuments, the whole lot belongs to the period prior to the annexation of Punjab by the British around the middle of the nineteenth century. There are scores of specimens of immovable antiquity having their origin in the years of the British Raj, and 'in existence for a period not less than seventy-five years'. But these somehow have escaped the eye or simply did not come within the scheme of the things earmarked by the Federal Government. Perhaps to make good this deficiency, the Punjab Government have also notified quite a number of immovable heritage within the Province. In order to keep a record of this period as far as Lahore is concerned, their lists have also been given, under Chapter III, as Annexure. A second monograph may also encompass their study in detail at some later date.

With the prevalent conditions of our government offices, it would have been well nigh impossible to gather together the record of all the protected antiquity if I had not been attached personally, around the middle of the 1980s, with a programme of sifting the old files to bring at one place the detailed documentation of the notifications right from the days of British India. Its credit must go to a very enterprising administrator in Archaeology, Shaikh Khurshid Hassan, who was then holding the charge of the post of the Director General in the Federal Department. The assignment was given to Salma Sultan Begum, then an Assistant Director in the Epigraphy Branch. I, in my capacity as the In-charge of the Publications Branch, oversaw her work and guided her in this project. She was almost through with the project when there was a change at the top. Quite in line with traditions in a developing country, fresh priorities and preferences came in to amend or stall most of the works or projects, which had been started by the old 'command', the protected-antiquity-record-gathering being one of them.

After some years, however, I saw a cyclostyled volume of this information but without any mention of the original workers and contributors, who had put in much of their labour to make it accessible. Moreover, the finished 'product' was full of errors and omissions betraying at the lack of interest – or competency – on the part of those, who were assigned to deliver it at this stage. Interestingly, for the present monograph, I had to go through a lengthy drill in approaching different quarters before I could gather the information on the 'left-over' antiquity to give a complete picture of the records. This exercise became lengthy and cumbersome because the Director (Headquarters) of the Directorate General of Archaeology and

Museums, Government of Pakistan (the most relevant and basic source of such information), informed that with the shifting of their premises the records were lying in 'hap-hazard' way and it might take some time to 'dig out' this information. This may reflect on the attitude and efficacy of the major official quarter, which feels shy in even sharing any information on antiquity. However, this attitude might perhaps go in to enhance the usefulness of this treatise, which is in your hands now.

Here the ingenuity of Chaudhry Niaz Ahmad must be appreciated, as it was he who made a pressing demand on me to work rather overtime to dig out all the necessary records and then write on these historical landmarks of Lahore after physical visits to them and making fresh assessment. With his input, not only that such a record will easily be available to any interested reader or a scholar but it might also serve the professionals and administrators in the field in formulating the future strategies for the preservation and maintenance of antiquity. I am thankful to him for being a source of inspiration at every step.

My grateful thanks also go to Chaudhry Afzaal Ahmad, who, like always, gave much of his time to see that the labour put in this project brought satisfying results at the end of the day. Similarly, Ali Kamran, a young but very enterprising professional, was also of immense help in many ways during the designing and printing of this monograph. I am grateful to him too for the troubles he took.

I must also offer my appreciative thanks to Talib Hussain and Tariq Masood, senior officers in the Punjab Archaeology, who, unlike most of my worthy colleagues in the Federal Department of Archaeology, were only too responsive to my queries and to make my access easy to the recorded – and printed – information. My friends, Abdul Azim and Iqbal Bhutta of the Northern Circle of Archaeology, Pakistan, also proved helpful, as did Afzal Khan and Sajjad Butt, in my search for knowledge. I acknowledge their help with thanks.

All the photographs/images included in this treatise were either taken by me or processed under my guidance. Amjad Javed, photographer of the Federal Archaeology was of immense help, in his private capacity, in the preparation of the desired results. I am thankful to him too. For the pictures depicting frescoes of Haveli Nau Nihal Singh, I am indebted to Humera Alam for her timely help.

The heart and soul put in the planning, designing and printing of this book will certainly be felt by the reader. The credit for this goes to Naseer Baluch, Farhana Rafique and their pomising team member, Aamir Ali. I am thankful to all of them.

It may be pointed that the order of the Landmarks appearing in this treatise follows a loose chronology as adhering to strict basis in time scale was not possible in view of quite a few of them with overlapping periods. At least in one case the protected landmark has been put in the list according to the date of its having been inscribed on the Protected List.

It may also be mentioned here that as the basic information on the protected antiquity has been taken from the recorded notifications so the names, abbreviations and scale of measurements – or even symbols for these units – and other data have been given as appearing originally. However, under the heading Explanations the equivalents of these units of measurement in the metric system have been given separately. The symbols used in the notifications for these units of measurement have also been explained for easy comprehension of those, who might not be familiar with them.

Lahore,
March 2006.

Ihsan H. Nadiem,
Former Director of Archaeology, Pakistan,
& Visiting University Professor of Architecture
Email: inadiem@yahoo.com

General view of the old city of Lahore.

Preamble I

Lahore, one of the most important cultural centres of the South Asia Subcontinent, is aptly known as the heart of Punjab while in its traditions and long chequered history it also has no rival in the whole of Pakistan. On the banks of the Ravi, which divides the Indus Plain from the lands of the Ganges, it played host or put up resistance to many an invader and conqueror coming from Central Asia, mostly pursuing their way to the heartland of the Subcontinent to subjugate and rule India.

The myth of its founding by Loh, a son of the legendary Rama or Ramchandra (c. 1200 to 800 BC) to take it back to the remote antiquity, does not get much support from the solid evidence on ground. The only monument to the event is a small and insignificant structure of the Temple of Loh, which incidentally came up, even that reportedly, only during the Sikh period in the first half of the nineteenth century of the Gregorian calendar. However, keeping in view the importance of the local legends, myths and lore of the remote past the conclusion about its belonging to the times of yore in that reference may not be easy to be set aside. Moreover, in no way the absence of archaeological evidence would suggest its blank period prior to the Christian era when there are numerous references in accounts of at least Alexander's adventure (some three and a quarter centuries before Christ). They clearly point towards the presence of a town or a city at this place. It is quite possible that this post on the River Ravi might not have the nomenclature of Lahore, as it is reckoned today, but still it points to its having existed even prior to that period.

Qutb-ud-din Aibak as king of the Indian possessions. The latter was thus crowned as the first Muslim sovereign of India at Lahore on July 24, 1205. Even though his capital was shifted to Delhi yet Lahore continued to be important as Darus Saltanat.

Although during the following periods when Punjab was under the rule of Mauryans and later on changed hands between a number of local and foreign rulers, Lahore must have been playing some role yet no particular mention is made till Sabuktagin's time. But as his son, Mahmud, started his multiple outings on this area, Lahore is mentioned quite frequently. It was then, during his period in the eleventh century A.D., that his confidant and lieutenant, Ayaz, was made governor of Lahore. It was during this era that the fort of Lahore is also mentioned as of mud-bricks, but on a higher plane than the city itself.

The physical manifestations of the period earlier than that of Qutbuddin Aibak, of the Slave Dynasty, are hard to find here for obvious reasons though it is cited in history in connection with the invasions and outings of other Ghaznavides and the Ghauris. On the death of Shahabuddin Muhammad Ghauri his nephew, Mahmud, assumed the title at Ghaur. He, however, invested Qutb-ud-din Aibak as king of the Indian possessions. The latter was thus crowned as the first Muslim sovereign of India at Lahore on July 24, 1205. Even though his capital was shifted to Delhi yet Lahore continued to be important as Darus Saltanat.

This city never went out of the limelight of history ever after. There is reason to believe that architectural contributions might have been made from that early time of the thirteenth century but they are hard to find now. The major contribution towards this end started with the coming to power of the second of the Mughal emperors, Humayun. There was then no looking back and excepting the short stint of the Pathan king, Sher Shah Suri, the specimens of built heritage spread over almost four centuries give the city reason to rightly boast of a very rich and unique cultural past.

However, the awareness to the importance of study, to record or to preserve the physical legacy was simply not there in the whole of the South Asia Subcontinent, till almost the middle of the nineteenth century, the time when it had already come under the British occupation. The humble beginning of the studies in archaeology and its allied branches had already been made, though on a limited scale – and that was also without any local effort – by some amateur British antiquarians, who had set up an organisation called Asiatic Society of Bengal in 1784. Obviously the ambit of its activities remained basically restricted to the areas in Bengal and to mostly privately owned epigraphic records. However, it was long after this that in 1862 the importance of this field had been recognised at official level and Sir Alexander Cunningham was appointed as 'Director of Archaeology'. The basic task given to him was 'to make accurate description of such remains as most deserve notice, with the history of them so far as it is traceable, and a record of the traditions that are retained regarding them'. There was no element of recognised permanence in the creation of this office; on the contrary, archaeological work was thought as something to be accomplished in a few years, duly recorded and then dropped.

By the year 1871 ideas on the subject had become somewhat more expanded. General Cunningham's appointment was declared, by a Resolution, to that of 'Director-General of the Archaeological Survey of India'. Now his duty was defined "to superintend a complete search over the whole country and a systematic record and description of all architectural and other remains that are remarkable alike for their antiquity, or their beauty, or their historical interest".

The responsibility of looking after, including repair and conservation, remained with the local governments till 1878. Lord Lytton brought this function into the fold of the Archaeological Survey and a Curator of Ancient Monuments – combining engineering with archaeological knowledge – was put in the position of an under-secretary in the Public Works Department, further to be assisted by a committee of taste, to undertake such works. Financial responsibility, continued to be that of the local governments, with additional funds from the Imperial grant.

After the retirement of Cunningham, Burgess was promoted to take his place in 1885. At this time the functions of conservation were amalgamated with those of survey and research. However, even at this stage there was no intention of making the Survey a permanent department. After Burgess, who retired in 1889, the Finance Committee of the Government of (British)

Lord Curzon, accepted the need of encouragement of research, the promotion of archaeological study, and the preservation of the relics of the past as "a part of our imperial obligation to India".

India appointed to overhaul expenditure in all branches of public service, commented on what they regarded as 'the unduly high cost of the Archaeological Survey'. This also resulted in keeping the post of Director General vacant, virtually abolished. Only the Provincial Surveyors were kept in three regions, the other five doing without such services. The Survey itself was sanctioned for five years starting from 1890, as it was thought that the work would be completed in the whole of India by that time. But the picture throughout this period remained gloomy, as gone were the Director General and Curators, bringing the research and upkeep of monuments at almost standstill.

At the end of the five-year period, in 1895, it became time for the Government to consider what the future of the Archaeological Department was to be. The Government of (British) India, on pleas from certain groups

Lahore city wall.

Lahore Fort: The temple of Loh. The architectural style betrays of its origin in the Sikh period.

came to the conclusion, but not before 1898, that it was neither possible to disband the Survey altogether, nor advisable to maintain it on its then reduced and ineffective scale. However, they laid more emphasis on conservation. The Survey was re-organised and expanded to spread over the whole of the (British) India.

Soon after his arrival in 1899 the new Viceroy of India, Lord Curzon, accepted the need of encouragement of research, the promotion of archaeological study, and the preservation of the relics of the past as "a part of our imperial obligation to India". He was, indeed, the man behind the fresh momentum of a long phase of awareness of the importance of the antiquity and the part it played in the lives of the peoples. Before the close of the year 1900, it had been felt that it would be the 'Supreme Government', and not the Provincial Governments, which would be primarily responsible for maintaining intact this great inheritance. They thought it unsafe to repose that trust in the subordinate governments in view of their limitations and restrained finances. These proposals were sanctioned by the Secretary of

State in the later part of 1901, and John Hubert Marshall was appointed as the new Director General for five years.

There were, however, no laws directly related to the protection and preservation of monuments. To meet certain legal requirements, merely some sections could be invoked in i) Bengal Regulation XIX of 1810, ii) Madras Regulation VII of 1817, iii) Act XX of 1863 (An act to enable the Government to divest itself of the management of Religious Endowments) and iv) Treasure Trove Act, 1878. The expansion in the activities in the field of recording, managing and conserving heritage treasures necessitated some legal framework to control and regulate actions in this sphere. It was with this background and, now, a strong will to secure and preserve the Heritage of the peoples of the Subcontinent that the government gave it the legal protection by enacting Ancient Monuments Preservation Act VII of 1904. Although it was then considered an adequate law on the subject yet further experience in the field called for enlargement in its statutory scope and was thus amended from time to time.

As the idea behind the work initiated in this discipline, which even in its vaguest sense might not have been recognized as such by then, was only to bring on record the antiquity for its architectural value, historical importance or simply magnificence. The prime interest of the pioneers – especially Cunningham – had remained glued to the study of ancient geography and holy places of the Buddhists in northern parts of the Subcontinent. With the recognition of its importance – and subsequent acts of giving it a permanent status – the work to register, preserve and administer antiquity took off over almost the whole of the British India. Lahore, with its unsurpassable treasures, was then no exception.

The architectural legacy of the Mughal period predominates the scene of our tangible cultural heritage in Lahore. And it is not without solid reasons. Not only that the Mughal dynasty ruled for the longest, most stable and very effective period in the history of the Subcontinent but also because Lahore being the most important station to thwart any attempt at the power from the west – or a necessary centre to keep control over the far-flung areas of the empire – served as the *Darus Saltanat*, literally headquarters of the empire though it remained the provincial capital, with Delhi/Agra serving as the seat of the government.

It thus had an ample share of the architectural and landscape legacy of the Mughals. Moreover, being one of the leading cities of South Asia

Lahore being the most important station to thwart any attempt at the power from the west – or a necessary centre to keep control over the far-flung areas of the empire – served as the Darus Saltanat,

Subcontinent, not only that the Mughal emperors and their retinues frequently visited Lahore, some Mughal princes and members of nobility also had a good taste of preference for this city to reside here for longer duration. Following the royalty, the *amirs, nawabs* and other classes of the elite also had their residences, *havelis* and gardens built here. Some of these landmarks have not only survived the vicissitudes and vagaries of time and man but also preserved their elegance and grandeur even after centuries of use or misuse and, often, long spells of neglect. The historic buildings in and, then, around the city did not fail to attract the official eye even at the early stages of recording the heritage during the British period. Most outstanding of these, indeed standing as landmarks, were protected from time to time under the Ancient Monuments Preservation Act of 1904, beginning with their notification from 1911.

By the time the Subcontinent attained independence from the British, and a new nation of Pakistan emerged on the world map on 14 August 1947, some 25 monuments had been notified as protected ones. Of these Landmarks only two belonged to the Pre-Mughal period, although none of them was in its remarkable or original shape. Some twenty-three (following the number of notifications – though 3 of the Kos Minars are seen as bracketed under one) of them were erected during the Mughal period. There were only two buildings originating in the Sikh period, which made part of the protected list of the pre-1947 days.

After independence as many as 31 monuments were notified in the meanings of the Ancient Monuments Preservation Act of 1904 as protected: some 23 of them pertain to the Mughal period, 5 belong to the Sikh era while there are 3, which were erected during the time-span that started after the fall of the Sikhs, more particularly during British Raj. These latest-mentioned ones, however, have been brought on the register because of their importance as National Monuments.

It is interesting to note that out of the 13 gates of the walled city only 6 stand protected and those too were notified during the year 1966, possibly treating them as the Mughal period remnants even if their present structures were almost thoroughly renovated, or even raised from ground, during the British period.

The Ancient Monuments Preservation Act of 1904 was replaced by the Antiquities Act of 1968, to bring the statute in line with the new realities of the independent Nation. However, in Lahore there is no antiquity on record,

It is now a hard fact of history that most of the gems of the architectural and landscape art existing in Lahore, and especially belonging to the Muslim period, were ruthlessly savaged by the Sikhs during their holding sway over the region.

which had been notified under this Act, which remained in force for about seven years.

The above-mentioned Act of 1968, in turn, was replaced by the Antiquities Act of 1975 (Act No. VII of 1976: An Act to repeal and re-enact the law relating to the preservation and protection of antiquities). This Act has also been amended from time to time as its implementation in the field brought to the fore some difficulties or else it was thought to improve upon its provisions. There are only two antiquities of the immovable nature, which have so far been protected under the Antiquities Act of 1975: one of them being the modern structure, the Islamic Summit Minar, termed as the National Monument while the other is the Tomb of Mir Niamat Khan that belongs to the Mughal era, Shah Jahan's period to be more precise.

It is now a hard fact of history that most of the gems of the architectural

Shalamar Gardens: Mela Chiraghan – the Fair of the Lights – used to be held inside the Mughal Gardens during the Sikh period and the early period of the British. It was spared of this irrelevant and highly damaging use only decades after its protection in 1913.

Shalamar Gardens: The white marble pavilion and other Mughal period architecture and garden features in shambles sometime during the early 20th century.

and landscape art existing in Lahore, and especially belonging to the Muslim period, were not only ruthlessly savaged by the Sikhs during their holding sway over the region from around the end of the 18th century to the middle of the 19th century but they also invented their most bizarre use resulting in ruination of some of the originality of the antiquity. It was of no consequence to them whether they used a historic mosque or a mausoleum as stable, treasury or given it to provide housing facility for some functionaries of the state. They robbed precious pieces or exquisitely done architectural elements and material from the grand buildings, especially of the Mughal period, to use thus pilfered-stuff elsewhere in their own built contributions. It is also on record that most of the stone used in the Golden Temple at Amritsar (now in Bharat) was also taken from Lahore by tampering some of the outstanding specimens of building art.

In no way perhaps their destructive acts like these ones, usually to adorn other buildings elsewhere, were the only scourges of the period. The war of succession of the later Sikhs also contributed towards the devastation of heritage representing some of the unique specimens of building art inside the Fort and the Badshahi Mosque. The matchlock men of Sher Singh occupied the minars when he besieged the Fort in 1841. Later on, light guns mounted on them bombarded the Fort, resulting in the ruination of many buildings including the Diwan-e-Aam, as Hira Singh was forcing out the besieged Sindhanwala Sirdars. The retaliation, in turn was the cause of much of the destruction, including that of the minars, of the Grand Mosque. After the Sikhs, the British simply continued with its former use as powder magazine. They, however, chose to carry out some repairs to the structures, especially the minarets, which had been hit by fire from inside the Fort. Interestingly, they sold the original red sandstone slabs to defray the cost of these repairs causing to the genuineness of the antiquity an irretrievable loss. When restored to the Muslims, the Mosque was still in shattered condition.

In an air of general apathy towards the vanquished at the earlier stages and an attitude of complacence about its historical, architectural, cultural or artistic values – or simply to follow the line of their strategic planning – the unique heritage suffered immensely at the hands of the British (Indian) government. Ironically, some of their acts led to the unmatched monuments greatly deprived of their originality or left them scarred through unethical and ugly-looking interventions, which in most of the places were also irreversible.

The major victim of this brutal attitude of the British rulers was no other than the Lahore Fort. Like all the invaders they were also apprehensive of the local people standing in revolt at any time. The Fort being very strategically situated and having the basic elements of defence could have been used

From the Hazuri Bagh Darwazah a curiously twisted passage led up to the western entrance of the great quadrangle of the Diwan-e-amm, which measured 730 by 460 feet, and was enclosed on four sides by a range of vaulted chambers with central gateways on the west, south and east sides.

against them. So they decided to destroy the invulnerability of the stronghold. The southern fortification wall was pulled down, replacing it with brick-steps, which would pose no hindrance to subdue the inmates by the attacking force in any eventuality. Another stepped gate with still easier steps to lead to the interior of the Fort was also constructed towards the western side of the same southern wall.

Perhaps not satisfied with these measures they also played havoc with the buildings located inside the Fort. In the words of J. PH. Vogel (writing for the Archaeological Survey of India Annual Report of 1911), "From the Hazuri Bagh Darwazah a curiously twisted passage led up to the western entrance of the great quadrangle of the Diwan-e-amm, which measured 730 by 460 feet, and was enclosed on four sides by a range of vaulted chambers with central gateways on the west, south and east sides. Of this large cloister nothing now remains except the little court in front of the Pearl Mosque. The front wall of this court formed part of the west side of the large enclosure, and still conveys some idea of its appearance. Its destruction for military purposes is more to be deplored by the antiquarian, as this arcade must have been one of the oldest portions of the Lahore palace".

To further erode defensive capability of the Fort, the Postern Gate was carved out, during 1853, through the western fortification of the Sikh period. The access to the interior of the Fort was further eased through this Gate by providing a road, capable of handling vehicular means including the carrying of the cannons, by making major interventions in the original plain.

Not only that the originality of the historic monument was compromised by these measures, but its secure nature was also ensured by mushroom-growth of barracks, even right at top of the western Fortification Wall, in addition to almost all over the open spaces – or even by making spaces open by removing some earlier structures. The two main Gates – Masti Gate and the Alamgiri Gate or what they called the Hazuri Bagh Gate – were bricked up while turning some of the elegant architectural specimens into Catholic chapel, church, hospital or simply residential or administrative quarters for the occupying force. Thankfully, after its transfer to the Archaeological Survey of (British) India most of the interventions – where possible – were undone, but certainly not without loosing some of the originality. Even the white-marble Diwan-i-Khas, to some the *Chhoti Khwab Gah* – or the smaller bedchamber – had to be dismantled and re-erected because of the deep-imbedded intrusions.

Thankfully, after its transfer to the Archaeological Survey of (British) India most of the interventions – where possible – were undone, but certainly not without loosing some of the originality. Even the white-marble Diwan-i-Khas, to some the Chhoti Khwab Gah – or the smaller bedchamber – had to be dismantled and re-erected because of the deep-imbedded intrusions.

The large water-tank with all its fountainheads, within the Jahangir's Quadrangle, had been filled up by the early British military to use the ground as a tennis court. It was retrieved to its original shape only after it came to the possession of the Archaeological Survey of India as a monument.

Even after most of the Old Fort was restored as antiquity, quite a few of its portions continued to be used by other departments of the Provincial government, having no relevance to the heritage, for a long time. The Basement Chambers of the Shish Mahal Complex were used as stores of the Civil Defence while the buildings in the southwestern corner, known as stables and kitchens in their original planning, remained under the occupation of the Police, where they had set up one of the most-dreaded 'jails' for hardened criminals and political prisoners or detainees. The chambers could be got vacated in early 1974 in the wake of Islamic Summit Conference during which a dinner in honour of the head of states and governments was to be hosted in the Shish Mahal. The interventions in the old structures to make it suitable for the occasion tell still another story of our flawed approach towards the heritage. The Fort even otherwise has remained the victim of official entertainment shows and celebrations in addition to a hosting ground for loud-functions of the ruling political parties, and never without suffering physical damage.

As to the area in the southwestern corner of the Fort under Police occupation, it was rescued from the incompatible use only in December 1986 and handed back to the Department of Archaeology, Pakistan, for restoration, which incidentally could never take effect. However, some of the Police barracks were later renovated and used to accommodate the newly set up Pakistan Institute of Archaeological Training and Research while some other buildings – mainly of the Sikh period – were made to give way to raise modern facilities to serve as a residential hostel, a conservation laboratory and a block of library. The professional competence – or the will and commitment behind it – could be gauged from the fact that most of these structures could not last till the next season and were thought to be dangerous for use. It would seem all the more ironical as the area still boasts of over a score of buildings erected more than 350 years ago.

Not only that the stone-facing of the Tomb of Nur Jahan was removed, now as usual, by the Sikhs they also dug even the two graves inside it on the presumption – or story in the air – that they contained precious jewels and jewellery belonging to the queen and her daughter. Some of the damage done to the interior of the Tomb was made good by Hakim Ajmal Khan, who

The chambers could be got vacated in early 1974 in the wake of Islamic Summit Conference during which a dinner in honour of the head of states and governments was to be hosted in the Shish Mahal

also put up a white marble plaque. The façade on the northern side was redone during the 1950s and 1960s with cement and colour, as the red sandstone was not locally available and posed difficulties in importing from India. However, the experiment did not give encouraging results and thus was not further extended. With the availability of the required stone at a later stage, the western façade has been redone in original pattern. The eastern and southern façades still present the pathetic condition it was left in by the Sikhs.

They had also not spared the jewel of architecture and landscaping – the Mausoleum of Jahangir – from where, in their quest for expensive material to adorn their own buildings, they removed whatever they could. Although there is a myth that they removed the superstructure from the Mausoleum yet a photograph of the British period does point out that at least something was left at the site by them at that time, which seems to have been completely annihilated during the British Raj.

In addition, in their turn the British also put in their share of destroying the Shahdara Complex of Monuments, the buildings and gardens of which once stood contiguous to each other. To lay the railway line towards Rawalpindi from Lahore, the connection between the Tomb of Nur Jahan and those of Asif Khan and Jahangir were severed forever. The historic monuments here were made to serve as railway stores depots.

The masterpiece of landscaping, Shalamar Gardens, also suffered immensely, first at the hands of the Sikh rulers – stripping it of its stones and precious decorations to reuse elsewhere – and then the unmindful British, especially the officers of their forces, who turned it into a picnic spot. It was its such use, as also the holding of the Mela Chiraghan inside it, which could be stopped only with a stern order from the higher echelons in the city.

The Lahore Fort and the Shalamar Gardens now stand inscribed on the List of World Cultural Heritage maintained by UNESCO, since 1982. Incidentally, these very monuments were also included in UNESCO's List of Endangered Cultural Property, due mainly to the ill-advised acts of omission and commission on the part of the Punjab Government, especially after it had bulldozed the Shahjahan period site of a well and the water-filtration arrangements of the Shalamar Gardens on the authority of the Chief Minister only to broaden the modern Grand Trunk Road. Ironically, now the administration and control of these World Heritage sites have been

Not only that the stone-facing of the Tomb of Nur Jahan was removed, now as usual, by the Sikhs they also dug even the two graves inside it on the presumption – or story in the air – that they contained precious jewels and jewellery belonging to the queen and her daughter

transferred to the very Provincial Government vide Government of Pakistan, Ministry of Minorities, Culture, Sports, Tourism and Youth Affairs Notification No.9-31/2000-A.II dated the 5th July, 2004.

The Extract from the UNESCO Record as to the inscription of the Lahore Fort and the Shalamar Gardens on World Cultural Heritage List and, later, the List of World Heritage in Danger appears as Annexure I, which speaks itself of the inability of the professionals to save the antiquity from its destruction at the whims of the authorities that be.

Still another glaring example of official apathy – at the cost of the cultural heritage – is the Survwala Maqbra, or the Tomb of Cypresses, where lies buried the most pious and accomplished daughter of Abdul Samad Khan, a governor of Punjab. It is the same Sharfun Nisa, who is the subject of Philosopher-Poet Allama Iqbal's poem in his Persian collection, Javed Namah. He extols her greatness by saying that her presence in Lahore had made its land stand at par with heavens. Then referring to the copy of the holy Quran and the sword that were kept in her grave, in accordance with her will, the Allama says that with their removal by the Sikhs, the Muslimhood has disappeared from Punjab.

As the relevant records show - while also the reports in the press that were never contradicted - the Auqaf department of the Government of the Punjab played havoc with it. According to the report published in 2004, the senior echelons of the Auqaf department made out residential plots of the 8 kanal Trust land belonging to the Tomb in 1989 and shared them among themselves, along with some, otherwise, well-known names in the Muslim religious luminary. The lease of the land was for 99 years at the paltriest amount of Rs.1.99 (Rupee one and paisas ninety-nine only). While some of them built houses on these plots, the others sold them at fabulously high prices. The report, referring to the Allama's poem, laments that even Sikhs, who removed the holy Quran and the sword from the grave structure, could not dare to occupy the land endowed to the Shrine. Not only that the Trust land was appropriated – under what law, the report writer feels at a loss to understand – the building of structures of the residential colony too close to the protected antiquity blatantly violated the provisions of the Antiquities Act 1975, which prohibits any such activity within 200 feet of the protected monument.

In an interesting development in the case, perhaps after its surfacing in the media, the allotments of Waqf (endowed) lands with the Auqaf Department

According to the report published in 2004, the senior echelons of the Auqaf department made out residential plots of the 8 kanal Trust land belonging to the Tomb in 1989 and shared them among themselves, along with some, otherwise, well-known names in the Muslim religious luminary.

Tomb of Noor Jahan: Still shows the pathetic condition it was left in by the Sikhs.

of the Punjab Government were cancelled through an Urdu letter from the office of the Chief Administrator, Auqaf Punjab, Lahore, addressed to Zonal Nazimeen (administrators) vide No.SOP-3(95)-Auqaf/62 dated 8 June, 2004. Also, with the Department of Archaeology, Pakistan, said to have already gone to the Court of Law, there does not seem to be any change on the ground even as late as 2006.

There are some other examples where the authorities not only failed to stop encroachments or destruction of the antiquity in Lahore, even though empowered – and otherwise required also – under law to protect them, they apparently seemed party to such actions. The very glaring case comes on record during the tenure of M. Ishtiaque Khan as Director General of Archaeology, Government of Pakistan. It started as a consequence of the issuing of NOC (No Objection Certificate) by him to a private party to construct a housing colony precariously close to the Complex of the Mausoleum of Emperor Jahangir, which to many scholars and architectural historians is perhaps the second most-outstanding Mughal feat – only after the Taj at Agra – portraying the best of planning and execution of a beauty of rare embellishment of all periods of history of the Subcontinent. Ironically, the rape of law – and with that of the heritage – by the very authority supposed to enforce it, could only be stopped by a private citizen, M. Rafique Dogar, by approaching the Federal Ombudsman (Wafaqi Mohtasib) to intervene in the matter. Thankfully, this institution rose to the occasion and made the authorities cancel the NOC thus saving one of the most precious antiquities getting scarred in the face while the whole of its backside (on the north) already has unauthorised – and ugly – structures built right against its high enclosure walls. The Order of the Federal Ombudsman (Wafaqi Mohtasib), which should also serve as guide to others in similar cases, is reproduced as Annexure II towards the end of this treatise.

There was still another case of the violation of the Law with fast coming up high-rise plaza in close proximity of the protected landmark of Chauburji. It, however, took a clandestine turn when allegedly interfered by some higher authority. The accused in that case is said to have hit back and got registered a case against some officials of the Department of Archaeology, Pakistan, who – he alleged – had got their 'share for co-operation'. They had to face ignominy of being in Police custody for some time, getting released only on bail later on. However, as the case is sub judice at this stage we may not be able to discuss it.

There are numerous examples of the complacent attitude of the officials, which is so graphically reflected by the present condition of the most of the protected monuments. The unenviable state of maintenance of the Islamic Summit Minar, which stands inscribed on the Protected list of the Federal Government as a National Monument, again speaks volumes about the official attitude. Not only that it is not maintained at an appropriate level, its projection in the 'useable area' is also pathetic. Presently it displays very casually, in free-standing glass-showcases, some specimens of ethnological material from certain Muslim countries, in addition to a very shabbily painted and written 'information board' and out-of-place models of 'Bab-e-Khyber" and the "Minar-e-Pakistan". The whole arrangement, and the way of its projection, is simply crude at the best. It warranted better treatment in view of its high place as National Monument. There was a proposal in the early 1990s to raise in this area a Museum of Muslim Coins for which the Numismatist In-charge of the Karachi's National Museum of Pakistan, Pervin

Ironically, the rape of law – and with that of the heritage – by the very authority supposed to enforce it, could only be stopped by a private citizen, M. Rafique Dogar, by approaching the Federal Ombudsman (Wafaqi Mohtasib) to intervene in the matter

Jahangir's Mausoleum: The superstructure, over the roof during British period – 1921.

Nasir, had also visited it and made on the spot studies. Whatever happened to this idea – or the scheme – is now anybody's guess.

The encroachments, albeit the presence of the Antiquities Act, have hardly left most of the landmarks of history in Lahore with an unhindered access, or even their clear view for the visitor or his camera.

As the Department of Archaeology, Government of Pakistan, restricted itself to the heritage of more representative nature, while also excluding any reference to most of the 'living' or Waqf (endowed) places, religious or secular, the Provincial authority promulgated "the Punjab Special Premises (Preservation) Ordinance, 1985" (XXXIV of 1985) and declared some 172 buildings in Lahore as "Special Premises" from 1985 to 1991 (a few of them though also having already been protected by the Federal Government).

However, the very fact that the list merely mentions the 'buildings' without giving any details – not even their locations or their value, which made them to be treated as such – speaks volumes of half-hearted move, though possibly with good intentions, made in the direction of better care and preservation of the priceless heritage. This step needed a continuously concerted follow up action in addition to formulating a definite policy in regard to these 'special premises' as almost all of them are 'living' areas very much in use even at present. Without an explicit policy and clear guidelines for the concerned authorities it would only be futile to expect them deliver the desired results.

Jahangir's Mausoleum: The roof with the platform suggesting one time presence of superstructure.

The religious premises – like shrines, mosques, temples, smadhs etc. – always remain in danger of obliteration of their genuineness or originality at the hands of the over-enthusiast devotees and the caretakers. No doubt they have their own concept of beauty, and they do create it by causing interventions, albeit irreversible, with decorative and expensive material like glass-mosaic, precious and semi-precious stones, paints etc. as also by adding, without any planning, inscriptional material and modern facilities like fans and airconditioners. In fact many of these have already lost their original substance and look. This state of affairs of their 'maintenance' could possibly hit at the high value of originality because of the lack of awareness and a considered and consistent policy. Their 'further' beautification and development could have also been executed without compromising with their originality only if proper planning had been made in consultation with the professionals.

The same would be true with commercial buildings, at a different plane though. In this age of competition they are always under threat of additions and alterations – even complete remodelling or reconstruction – to meet the challenges of staying in business and prospering. All these constraints must have been taken into account and given serious thought while enacting the relevant legislation aimed at preserving the historical, cultural or architectural values of such premises.

It is somewhat heartening that the Punjab Government, very recently, have made certain efforts to keep a check on unilateral interventions of these premises by their owners or administrators, as far as commercial buildings are concerned. Some of them are on record to have been made to get a No Objection Certificate before undertaking any such project in hand. (It is another thing that the Provincial Government itself did not adhere to the conservation principles in the past. We have before us some blatant examples like the destruction of the Water Filtration Complex of the Shalamar – belonging to the period of Shah Jahan – at the orders of the Chief Minister to widen the G.T.Road; the 'over-restoration' of Kamran's Baradari – the very first of the surviving feat of the Mughals at Lahore – and development of a complex at the Shrine of Hazrat Data Ganj Bakhsh completely ignoring the importance of the old structures). With a somewhat marked change in the attitude of the government towards the built heritage, the involvement of the Local Government in this endeavour must bring positive results in saving these 'Special Premises' from getting scarred, altered or even obliterated only if these authorities themselves are aware of the prized importance of their originality.

However, to save these manifestations of our cultural achievements both the Federal and the Provincial Governments would have to make such rules regulations or guidelines, which could be practical and sustainable while responsible authorities easily accessible by the private parties, who are looking after these places of reverence

However, to save these manifestations of our cultural achievements both the Federal and the Provincial Governments would have to make such rules, regulations or guidelines, which could be practical and sustainable while responsible authorities easily accessible by the private parties, who are looking after these places of reverence. Moreover, the authorities will have to endeavour to develop educational programmes and media campaigns, at the national level, informing the public about the importance of the heritage.

Human plunder and neglect apart, monuments also fall easy prey to weathering agents when time has already given serious blow to their shell and fabric. Humidity by far is the major enemy attacking the buildings through capillary action. The mushroom growth of residential colonies and all sorts of buildings around these monuments have affected adversely the natural flow of rain, or even sewer, water, which now attacks these landmarks of history and badly damages by accumulating through seepage in the thickness of the walls. It naturally results in faster disintegration of the faces of the walls, and at a later stage, weakening of the roofs.

There are also some other genuine difficulties in the face of the will to achieve the aim of better-upkeep of these historic landmarks. In line with the character of developing countries the cultural heritage attracts but only the lowest priority with the powers that be. No wonder then that serious problems and difficulties have been faced in proper maintenance and preservation of the time-worn, human-plundered and long neglected antiquities. Like everywhere else in Pakistan, the speed of deterioration in the Historic Landmarks of Lahore has also been faster than that of the conservation measures, where these could be taken, to arrest the decay. It has obviously multiplied the volume of work to be attended to with the passage of time while the effective value of the resources has continuously been eaten up by the never-ending inflation.

During the early days of independence not much financial support was available to undertake any major operation in the field of conservation and preservation of antiquity. The work on restoration of earlier features – that too only of the more important monuments – continued bit by bit for much of the time. For many years, just a paltry sum continued to be allocated on yearly basis, which was squarely insufficient to meet the minimum cost of their maintenance, even in respect of the more important monuments. Even after the introduction of preparing Master Plans, and getting funds on their approval since the early 1970s, the fortune did not smile their way due mainly to the slow release of the chunks of money and that too mostly

Human-plundered and long neglected antiquities. Like everywhere else in Pakistan, the speed of deterioration in theHistoric Landmarks of Lahore has also been faster than that of the conservation measures, where these could be taken, to arrest the decay.

towards the end of the Financial Year.

With the Cultural Heritage at almost the lowest rung of priorities of the Ministry of Finance, the nature of funds allocated on yearly basis, being lapsable at the end of the financial year, has affected much adversely on their proper utilisation. The inherent 'slow-moving' nature of the employees coupled with long procedural methods to undertake any work, go in to see that only a part of the budgetary allocation is utilised judiciously. Thus either the funds lapse or else are utilised in such a hasty manner as to diminish much of their utility, often also resulting in compromising with the set conservation practices. This nature of the resources was spelled out as the main cause of unsatisfactory results in the preservation of antiquity by Sir Bernard Feilden, Director Emeritus of ICCROM and an internationally acknowledged giant in the field of conservation of architectural heritage. He had made special studies of the Built Heritage of Pakistan in 1989, to record the reasons behind their fast deteriorating condition. Among other reasons this drawback of the system was treated by him as of fundamental nature. With the sole aim to overcome this basic difficulty, he had suggested the creation of a Fund on the lines of the English Heritage. With much of his input and after thorough study of the examples of the kind, a skeletal draft was prepared by the author of this treatise. It went through the required channels – with their inputs – ultimately resulting in the creation of the National Fund for Cultural Heritage in 1994.

The authorities that controlled the Fund became more conscious of multiplying the net sum by uninterrupted investment rather than spending for the betterment of the Heritage, which incidentally was its real aim, especially targeting the major problem of availability of funds and their lapsing nature at the end of the year

However, when it became operative after enactment as Act, it also fell to our typical system and flawed priorities, which helped beat the usefulness of the exercise thus defeating the basic reason behind the creation of such a Fund. The authorities that controlled the Fund became more conscious of multiplying the net sum by uninterrupted investment rather than spending for the betterment of the Heritage, which incidentally was its real aim, especially targeting the major problem of availability of funds and their lapsing nature at the end of the year. The grants from it were given, sporadically, for different projects, not necessarily connected directly with the maintenance or conservation of the built heritage. (The Annexure IV, towards the end of this book, gives a summary of the projects funded by the NFCH, which gives a general perception of the Heritage Fund utilisation strategy adopted so far).

However, when in an exceptional case they were obliged to part with some mentionable chunk they started a systematic campaign and were able to prove the right very wrong thus even discouraging the sincere professionals to take in hand any such project lest their own careers would be in jeopardy. From the present state of maintenance and preservation of antiquity it is very obvious that the vicious circle that be has prevailed over all the considerations of saving the heritage and in spite of the addition in the means these manifestations of our glorious past continue to suffer because of a very pronounced indifference towards them. It continues to be their fate even if Funds seem to be available at present.

The major impediment – the shortage of funds and their lapsable nature – could be removed if the whole of the budgetary allocations now given to the concerned Government Departments, along with all the Gate Money earned from the Monuments, are deposited into the account of the National Fund for Cultural Heritage and they, in turn, meet the charges on the maintenance, conservation, restoration etc. of our physical legacy. The disjointed proposals of so called documentation and collecting and acquiring 'cultural material', so very popular themes mostly with the NGOs and individuals with right connections, should be discouraged in the larger interest of the preservation, restoration and maintenance of the monuments. It would need only rethinking and re-aligning of their priorities though the more important factor that would count towards a positive progress would certainly remain the will of the authorities to serve the national heritage. Only well established practising institutions and departments should be brought in this fold to bring up their i) short term and ii) long term conservation/ restoration proposals. It would not seem advisable to expose more antiquity to danger of obliteration – or spend fund in fields other than its saving – unless something could be done about the existing ones. It also seems very necessary that for the running of the NFCH, professionals, who have practical experience in field and are not mere academicians – or sheer art lovers for that matter - should be brought in the decision-making positions if there still remains any will to save the legacy of the Nation.

Leaving aside the apathy of the concerned officials – some of them also tell of their limitations in such cases – the utter absence of awareness of the importance of the heritage on the part of common citizen – or many of the Nauveau-riche even if otherwise 'educated – is indeed lamentable, to say the least. This situation seems to be the outcome of the water-tight-compartment working of the concerned departments and organisations, which have failed over the scores of decades in instilling the sense and the realisation on the importance of the heritage in the minds of the general public – by and large not educated on the subject. Barring a few, who have taken upon themselves to popularising the subject with their personal efforts

To achieve any degree of success in ending the destruction of our shared cultural heritage and undiscovered past it is very necessary that public awareness is raised

over the media, the majority of the professionals – or even the non-governmental organisations – have an indifferent attitude or, at the most, the arm-chair approach, to the infested problem. To achieve any degree of success in ending the destruction of our shared cultural heritage and undiscovered past it is very necessary that public awareness is raised, as also hinted at elsewhere, by developing educational programmes and media campaigns informing the public about the misuse – or improper use – of these monuments and their environment, which is avidly detriment to the cause of the heritage. In the present scenario all those who matter in this field, in stead of reaching out to the common populace, normally suffice to pay courts to the power that be or heavily depend on holding meetings in a fashionable way. This 'strategy', even with much stretched imagination, cannot bring home any solution that could help ease the situation and, in the end, save these historic landmarks to hand them over to posterity.

In the present scenario all those who matter in this field, in stead of reaching out to the common populace, normally suffice to pay courts to the power that be or heavily depend on holding meetings in a fashionable way.

The Protected Landmarks

Aibak's Tomb: General view of the modern building.

Qutbuddin Aibak, the Slaves Dynasty Sultan of India and a successor of Shahabuddin Ghauri died as a result of fall from a horse while playing Chaugan (Polo) in 1210 AD and was buried in the area now known as Anarkali Bazaar, the well-known market place of Lahore

1. Name of Monument: **Qutbuddin Aibak's Tomb.**

a) Owned and maintained by   Government (DAP)
b) Category/Classification   I

c) Character & Date/Period	Muslim Religious/ Early 13th century/late 20th century AD.
d) Whether demarcated	Yes
e) Area	25.5 Marlas
f) Number & date of Notification:	No. 385/ dated: 6.4.1914.

DESCRIPTION:

Qutbuddin Aibak, the first of the Slaves Dynasty Sultan of India and a successor of Shahabuddin Ghauri died as a result of fall from a horse while playing *Chaugan* (Polo) in 1210 AD and was buried in the area now known as Anarkali Bazaar, the well-known market place of Lahore. This area in those days was an expansive open ground or a garden and it is said that it was here that he was playing Polo. However, with very scanty information on the subject it cannot be said with any certainty that a tomb-structure was erected on his grave. It becomes all the more controversial in the light of the mention of only '*qabr*' (grave) in the Tabqat-e-Akbari. The scholars thus conclude that it might have been left without any formal building over it. However, in Tahqiqat-e-Chishti it is mentioned that there was a marble tomb, which was pulled down by Ranjit Singh. But an archaeological probe in the form of trial trenches made at the site during the 1950s gave no indication of any structure of reasonable dimensions over the place to suggest the presence of a tomb or a mausoleum.

As leaving the site with an unpretentious grave over the remains of the first Sultan, who established the Muslim rule in the South Asia Subcontinent, was taken as an apathetic gesture by the general public, it was decided by the Government of Pakistan to acquire the land around the grave to design and erect a tomb-building in the white marble taking the cue from the famous historian of Tahqiqat-e-Chisti. As such in this

In Tahqiqat-e-Chishti it is mentioned that there was a marble tomb, which was pulled down by Ranjit Singh. But an archaeological probe in the form of trial trenches made at the site during the 1950s gave no indication of any structure of reasonable dimensions over the place to suggest the presence of a tomb or a mausoleum

Aibak's Tomb: Details of marble jail and grave.

congested area only two houses round the grave were acquired and a plan for the construction of a fresh but befitting tomb was prepared by the Department of Archaeology, Pakistan. The work on it was started in 1971 while it was completed in 1984. Although effort seems to have been made to incorporate architectural features of the Sultanate period yet the overall impact of the new building suggests that not much research and ground work were done before embarking on such a project. The mausoleum looks a bit taller in relation to its dimensions as well as the environment in which it has been built.

The site, with no eye on the unwieldy traffic in the narrow-lane approach, is additionally choked and presents an ugly scene with vehicles parked against its low boundary wall.

Aibak's grave within residential buildings before the area was acquired for development. Photo:1931.

Tomb of Musa Ahangar.

2.   Name of Monument: Tomb of Musa Ahangar, Mosque and House.

a) Owned and maintained   by Government (DAP)
b) Category/Classification   I
c) Character & Date/Period   Muslim, Lodhi Dynasty/ (1451-1526 AD)
d) Whether demarcated   Yes
e) Area   19M, 100F, 1M, 2M, 102F.
f) Number & date of Notification: No. F.5-6/65-A&M,
                                 dated: 6.4.1914.

DESCRIPTION:

About 600 yards (about 550 metres) southwest of Lahore Railway Station is the oldest Mughal building in Lahore outside the fortress. The structure,

Mosque of Musa Ahangar, now completely renovated and rebuilt.

It is the only surviving example of the craft of tile-work practised at Lahore before the period of Shahjahan. Its plain four-centred arches and the complete absence of tile-mosaic and of colours other than blue or blue-green and white are usually taken by scholars as the positive and negative features, which alike emphasize its early date.

which measures only 25 feet square externally, is traditionally the burial-place of a certain Sheikh Musa Ahangar, who, according to the Ain-e-Akbari (late sixteenth century), was living early in Akbar's reign. The attribution is not explicitly confirmed, but the *Tughra* characters of the Quranic inscription in the interior, and the design of the building itself, are consistent with a date in the second half of the sixteenth century.

Externally, the walls are panelled. The panels contain four-centred arches and appear to have been plastered. In each side is a four-centred doorway but modern blocking and replacement obscure the original details. The squat dome, its cylindrical drum, and the upper part of the façades are tiled. The green enamelled tiles of the dome are set horizontally with the rest having square tiles put diagonally and bearing floral patterns in white and blue. There is the battlement cresting provided round the top of the drum. Internally, the building is plastered and panelled, with elaborate tracery and arabesques in relief on the panels and in the spandrels of the squinches, which carry the dome. They seem to have originally been painted though presently the paint appearing on them does not seem to be original. There are niches adorned with decorative plasterwork in each of the west, north and south walls. The grave is a simple brick construction finished with plaster and whitewashed.

The tomb, otherwise an unpretentious building, owes its importance from the fact that it is the only surviving example of the craft of tile-work practised at Lahore before the period of Shahjahan. Its plain four-centred arches and the complete absence of tile-mosaic and of colours other than blue or blue-green and white are usually taken by scholars as the positive and negative features, which alike emphasize its early date.

Lately, the tomb structure has been turned into a make-shift mosque by blocking the door and turning the place into a sort of hall. Outside the building usual modern day piping has been fixed to hang electric fans for the convenience of the Faithful offering their prayers in the open during summer time.

Similarly, the mosque, said to have been built contemporaneously with the Tomb, has almost changed its whole look. Except for a few negligible indications, it appears as almost the whole new structure with usual feature of the provision of the shops on the outer side.

Lately, the tomb structure has been turned into a make-shift mosque by blocking the door and turning the place into a sort of hall. Outside the building usual modern day piping has been fixed to hang electric fans for the convenience of the Faithful offering their prayers in the open during summer time.

Kamran's Baradari after over-restoration.

3. Name of Monument: Mirza Kamran's Baradari.

a) Owned and maintained by	Government (DAP)
b) Category/Classification	I
c) Character & Date/Period	Muslim Secular
	1530-1540 AD
d) Whether demarcated	No
e) Area	6.53 Acres (68k-4m)
f) Number & date of Notification:	No. 22350
	Dated: 18.6.1935.

DESCRIPTION:

Constructed by Mirza Kamran, the eldest son of Babar around 1530 AD, it is the first Mughal structure at Lahore, which presents one of the earliest summerhouses built at Lahore. Apart from his political debacles the Prince, Mirza Kamran, was a very accomplished man of his age. He was pioneer of landscape architecture, especially a Mughal styled garden at Lahore, which could be called the forerunner of numerous others that came afterwards in different parts of the Empire. The *Baradari* (pavilion), now the only surviving evidence of this vast complex, was in the centre of a garden about 1,600 feet square. The recreation garden also had a number of other pavilions and a perimeter wall. The present Baradari originally stood in the centre of a high tank, and was approached by causeways.

This summerhouse has not only played host to a number of Mughal monarchs and princes during earlier 200-year history (1540-1740) but also witnessed some of the historical events of the rare nature. It was here that the rebellious prince Khusrow, after his capture by the royal pursuer on Chenab while fleeing to Kabul, was presented to Emperor Jahangir. The two close associates of the Prince were put in animal skins and let to die here. The Prince himself was made to witness the 700 other traitors punished to death by piercing alive on the sharp poles fixed in a double row from the Garden of Kamran to the gates of Lahore.

The garden originally stood a little distance from the right bank of the River Ravi, but its ravages have destroyed everything except a 'baradari' and some other features, which now make an island within the river-course. Whatever was spared by the river, the Punjab Government under Chief Minister Shahbaz Sharif, in its enthusiasm to restore the monument to its past glory, caused to tamper with its originality, though making it look more beautiful from the contemporary standards.

Kamran's Baradari, destroyed by the Ravi and neglect.

Lahore Fort showing Jahangir's Quadrangle. Also visible are Barri Khwabgah and recovered tank, which was filled to make a tennis court by the British.

4. Name of Monument: **Old Fort**

a) Owned and maintained by	Government (DAP)
b) Category/Classification	I
c) Character & Date/Period	Muslim, Secular (2nd half of 16th to 17th century AD. A few Sikh buildings of 1st half of 19th century AD)
d) Whether demarcated	Yes
e) Area	43.8 Acres
f) Number & date of Notification:	No. 11078/dt. 9.4.1924 No. 2524/dt. 27.1.1920

DESCRIPTION:

Early history of the Fort is shrouded in mystery and nothing definite is known about it. Traditionally it is stated that the Fort was built as early as the city itself and its foundation attributed to mythic Loh, a son of the hero of Ramayana of legendary Age (1200 – 800 BC). A small shrine known as the temple of Loh still exists in Lahore Fort, near the Alamgiri Gate, which gives support to this tradition, in spite of the fact that it was built as late as the nineteenth century during the Sikh reign.

Lahore Fort: Sikh period Athdara and superstructure. Also seen is the 2005-structure erected during restoration of Shish Mahal.

The authentic mention of the Fort is found in connection with Muhammad Sam's invasion of Lahore in 1180 AD, although it was rebuilt later by Emperor Balban in 1267 AD. In its present shape, it was built by Akbar the Great in 1566 AD, when he replaced the earlier mud-brick masonry with burnt brick construction, while also enlarging it considerably.

The contribution of Akbar the Great in the construction of the Fort is referred to in the Ain-e-Akbari in the following words: "Lahore is a large city in the Bari Doab. In size and population it has few rivals. In old books it is called Lahawar. In this everlasting reign the Fort and palace have been built of burnt bricks. As it was for some time the seat of Government, lofty edifices were erected and delightful gardens added to its beauty."

For establishing its origin, with conclusive evidence, excavations were carried out in the Fort by the Department of Archaeology of the Government of Pakistan, in the open lawn in front of Diwan-i-Am in 1959. A trench measuring 180 by 60 feet was laid and the digging was executed down to a depth of 50 feet where the natural soil was encountered. As a result twenty stratified cultural layers were brought to light, which from top to bottom on the natural soil, formed four distinct periods. These periods represented, one following the other, the British and Sikh, Mughal, Pre-Mughal and the Pre-Muslim.

Below the levels of the pre-Mughal period the remains of non-Muslim or Hindu period were brought to light. The beginning of period I was marked by the appearance of 7 feet thick layer of debris mixed with fallen mud bricks indicating great disturbance. The clearance of this thick deposit revealed a 12 feet high wall of mud bricks against which much cultural debris had accumulated. This may represent the non-Muslim mud-brick Fort of the yore.

Lahore Fort is the only place in Pakistan, which represents the different phases in the development of Mughal architecture. It achieved prominence during the reign of Emperor Akbar. Afterwards his successors, Jahangir, Shahjahan and Aurangzeb added numerous new buildings. The architecture of Akbar's period in the Fort is mainly in red sandstone with the combination of beam and bracket. More or less the same architecture is witnessed in the buildings of Jahangir's era as he continued to complete many a work commenced by Akbar, and added his own probably keeping them on the same lines. Shahjahan, who was known as Prince Architect of South Asia gave Lahore Fort some of the highly decorated and embellished buildings.

Below the levels of the pre-Mughal period the remains of non-Muslim or Hindu period were brought to light. The beginning of period I was marked by the appearance of 7 feet thick layer of debris mixed with fallen mud bricks indicating great disturbance. The clearance of this thick deposit revealed a 12 feet high wall of mud bricks against which much cultural debris had accumulated. This may represent the non-Muslim mud-brick Fort of the yore.

Lahore Fort: The white marble "Jharoka" or the "Takht" of Akbar's Diwan-e-Khass-o-Aam, opening into the later period Shahjahan's Diwan-e-Aam or the Hall of Forty Pillars.

The Fort is situated at the northwest corner of the city. It is irregular in plan being about 500 yards east to west by some 400 yards north to south. A fortification wall, constructed in small burnt bricks having considerable strength, girdles it all around. At intervals the wall has got bastions and loopholes for musketry. However, during the British period, before handing it over to the Archaeological Survey, the fortification, among other alterations, on the southern side was pulled down and turned in to a set of large stairs so as to weaken its utility as a defence wall.

The important buildings of the fort are Dault Khana-e-Khas-o-Am, Sleeping

Lahore Fort: Details of Red Sandstone carved brackets of Jahangir's Quadrangle.

An aerial view of the Hazuri Bagh, Lahore Fort and beyond. A number of monuments located within these premises are easily recognizable.

Chamber of Emperor Jahangir, Shish Mahal, Diwan-e-Am, Diwan-e-Khas, Moti Masjid, Alamgiri Gate, etc. etc.

Roshnai Gate seen far back in relation with Hazuri Bagh.

5. Name of Monument: Roshnai Gate.

a) Owned and maintained by   Government (DAP)
b) Category/Classification   I
c) Character & Date/Period   Muslim Secular
                                    1566 AD
d) Whether demarcated   Yes
e) Area   2.38 Acres (32k-19m)
f) Number & date of Notification: No.2906/ISG/Arch
                                            Dated 25.1.1935

DESCRIPTION:

Roshnai Gate is the earliest gate of the fortification wall built by Emperor Akbar around 1566 AD. It has also many historical associations. It was a

Roshnai Gate, viewed from north. Also seen is the Sikh period monument built against it.

gate, which was kept illuminated throughout the night during the Mughal period and it was through this gate that the big caravans entered the Serai that came to be known as Hazuri Bagh from the time of Ranjit Singh. It was here that Nau Nihal Singh, the third Sikh ruler of Ranjit Singh's lineage died because of the collapse of a portion of its arch.

Maryam Zami Mosque, also seen in the back are Masti Gate and the east fortification of the Fort. Parts of minarets and domes of the Badshahi Mosque are also visible in the far background.

6. Name of Monument: Maryam Zamani (or Begum Shahi) Mosque.

a) Owned and maintained by	Private
b) Category/Classification	I
c) Character & Date/Period	Muslim, Religious/ AH 1023 / 1614 AD
d) Whether demarcated	Yes
e) Area	6K-7M (195 sft)
f) Number & date of Notification:	No. SRO.1038(k)/62 Dated 30.4.1963.

DESCRIPTION:

On the eastern side of the Fort, almost against the Akbar period Gate – commonly known as Masti Gate - lies the earliest-dated mosque of Lahore. It was founded by Maryam Zamani Begum, mother of Emperor Jahangir and sister of Amirul Omara Raja Bhagwan Das, in AH 1023 /1614 AD, as recorded in an inscription consisting of three couplets fixed on the northern gateway.

The chronogram – transliterated as '*khush Masjeday*', in English meaning 'what a fine mosque' – gives the date. The Mosque is also known as Barud

Khaneh Wali Masjid because Ranjit Singh used its premises as a gunpowder factory. It was restored to the Muslims in 1850 AD during the British Raj.

It is a simple but massive structure of moderate size of a style transitional between the Pathan and the Mughal. The prayer chamber, which is 130'-6" long 34' deep, is divided into five compartments by means of thick arches supported on massive jambs. It bears five domes - not three as stated by Syed Muhammad Latif and Mortimer Wheeler. The central dome is larger and higher, while placed on a high neck. This is the earliest existing double dome not only at Lahore but also in whole of Pakistan. The lower shell is almost purely of 'guchh' (stucco). Wooden uprights about 3" x 3" in section standing between the upper and lower shells with their ends embedded in them are a curious feature. It appears that the builders used them as a means of reinforcement. The interior of the central dome is decorated with *Ghalibkari* (interlaced ribbing and panelling) with small cards at points of intersection inscribed with attributes of God in good calligraphy. The interior of the four smaller domes was perhaps also treated with *Ghalibkari*, but now it is plastered and white washed. The central dome has honeycombed squinches and the rest four with inconspicuous pendentives. On the roof, the four corners of the prayer chamber have unusual low square arched towers or pavilions surmounted by small cupolas on octagonal drums.

The prayer chamber with its five four-centred openings, the central as usual being larger, framed and provided with a half dome, open into a courtyard measuring 123' x 83' with a water tank - 31'-5" x 26'-3" - in its centre. The eastern portion of the courtyard measuring about 17' in width is now occupied by a platform of later date and a modern tomb stands in the northeast corner where there are traces of an old staircase leading to the roof. The original compound wall was niched and panelled as can be seen in the northeast corner. The main entrance of the Mosque is on the east, but there is a subsidiary one on the north. The entire flooring is modern.

The building is of little architectural note, but its importance lies in the excellent paintings or coloured decorations, which are an example of artistic work locally known as '*Munnabatkari*'. It is composed of very low incised-and-relief work, almost of paper thickness, on a common background.

It is unrivalled, at least, in Pakistan for sobriety in tone, variety of designs - both floral and geometrical - and delicacy. The panels include cypresses, palms, other trees and creepers, flowerpots etc. generally framed in elaborate geometrical patterns.

Presently the monument is heavily surrounded by a mushroom growth of modern structures almost encroaching upon such an important mosque that is unique in age. Equally fussy and tedious is its approach from the main road, opposite the Masti Gate, where an ensemble of eyesore shops of old parts of machinery and vehicles has come up in recent years.

The Mosque is also known as Barud Khaneh Wali Masjid because Ranjit Singh used its premises as a gunpowder factory. It was restored to the Muslims in 1850 AD during the British Raj

Tomb of Anarkali.

7. Name of Monument: Tomb of Anarkali

a) Owned and maintained by   Government (DAP)
b) Category/Classification   I
c) Character & Date/Period   Muslim, Religious/
                                    AH 1024 (1615 AD)
d) Whether demarcated   Yes
e) Area
f) Number & date of Notification: No. 11078, dated 9.4.1924.

DESCRIPTION:

Anarkali (pomegranate bud) is the attributed name, because of her beauty, of Nadira Begum or Sharfun Nisa brought up in the Harem of Emperor Akbar. It is said, she was suspected by the Emperor of carrying on a secret love affair with Prince Salim, afterwards to become Emperor Jahangir. The story is variously told, but the pith of the legend is that the poor girl was executed for her amorous folly in 1599 AD. Six years later, when Salim came to the throne he, in the memory of his beloved, got erected this big and bold monument over her remains.

The mausoleum, which stands within the enclosure of the Punjab Civil Secretariat, was completed in 1615 AD. In Mughal times it was surrounded by an extensive garden enclosed by a wall with a double storey gateway, now altogether missing. It underwent so many changes from time to time while serving various purposes - from residence to a chapel - during the respective periods of the Sikhs and the British that it has lost all its original decorations. In 1891 AD it was converted into Punjab Records Office, which purpose it still serves even today.

The marble cenotaph is elaborately carved with delicate floral and tendril designs, though the lines of carvings are not sharp. The calligraphy is in *Nastaliq*, boldly carved, but it lacks in uniformity of pen. On the top and three sides are inscribed 99 attributes of God. Besides, there is a hemistich on each side of the cenotaph.

The other two inscriptions give the date of death (of Anarkali) both in figures and words as 1599 AD and the date of the construction of the tomb as 1615 AD.

But nowhere on the monument or on the tombstone the name of the person whose mortal remains this mausoleum contains is mentioned. This may be so because nowhere Anarkali or her story is mentioned in history, but no doubt the tomb in question is traditionally known after her. The quality of the calligraphic work, as mentioned above, together with the style in which the name of the Prince – Salim bin Akbar, certainly not in vogue then with the royalty in India – do point to some serious omission. To the writer of this monograph it would appear to have been faked later on to give coin to an imaginary story. However, the architectural evidence is enough to place it as an important monument in the cultural history of Lahore.

The building, octagonal in plan with alternate sides measuring 44' and 30'-4" respectively, stands on an octagonal platform 163' long. On each corner, there is a domed octagonal tower, and in the centre, there is a huge dome standing on high cylindrical neck. The notable feature of the tomb is its huge massive structure with upper storey gallery and bold outlines. It is one of the earliest existing examples of double domed structure in Pakistan. The lower shell of the dome is constructed in small bricks in five stages or rings, marking a stage in the evolution of properly radiated lower dome, completed finally in the Taj at Agra.

The marble cenotaph is elaborately carved with delicate floral and tendril designs, though the lines of carvings are not sharp. The calligraphy is in *Nastaliq*, boldly carved, but it lacks in uniformity of pen. On the top and three sides are inscribed 99 attributes of God. Besides, there is a hemistich on each side of the cenotaph

Tomb of Prince Perwaiz: General view.

8. Name of Monument: Tomb of Prince Perwaiz

a) Owned and maintained by	Government (DAP)
b) Category/Classification	I
c) Character & Date/Period	Muslim, Religious/
	AH 1036 (1626 AD)
d) Whether demarcated	No
e) Area	3K-2M
f) Number & date of Notification:	No. F.17-107/55-Estt,
	Dated: 27.8.1956.

DESCRIPTION:

Prince Perwaiz was a son of Emperor Jahangir. He died in Lahore AH 1026 (1626 AD) and was buried in Chah Miran area. During the Mughal period, this place was called Perwaizabad and it was a city-quarter with a flourishing market. This tomb was most probably constructed by Shahjahan because it was after only two years when Shahjahan came to the throne. It is an irregular type of tomb, which stands on an octagonal platform supported by arches. The dome has a very high drum and this makes the entire structure very much elegant. In the architectural style it comes very near to the tomb structures in Iran.

Tomb of Mahabat Khan with boundary wall.

9. Name of Monument:

Tomb of Mahabat Khan and Boundary Wall (Baghbanpura)

a) Owned and maintained by	Government (DAP)
b) Category/Classification	II
c) Character & Date/Period	Muslim, Religious/ c. AH 1044/1634 AD
d) Whether demarcated	No
e) Area	Tomb platform (50' x 50'-2") Boundary wall (W. 250', N.118"-1", S. 159', E. ....) Open ground including tomb (9K17M/ 212 sft).
f) Number & date of Notification:	No. F.17-66/55-Estt., dated 6.8.1956.

DESCRIPTION:

The monument lies in Baghbanpura towards the left of the road as one proceeds to Shalamar Garden from the city of Lahore. It now hardly presents the pristine glory. There are the remains of the panelled and niched enclosure walls on west and partially on north and south with original gate on west on which a second storey was added by a Parsi Merchant of Bombay in the 19th century. In the centre there is a brick built platform with a brick built grave, which is said to be that of Mahabat Khan surnamed Khan-e-Khanan Yaminud Daula whose original name was Zamana Baig and who was a noble and commander of forces during the respective reigns of Jahangir and Shahjahan. According to Oriental Biographical Dictionary of Beals, he died in AH 1044/ 1634 AD in Deccan but his corpse was conveyed to Delhi and buried there. It, therefore, brings in many doubts about the myth of his having been buried here.

It is, however, probable that the garden, which once stood here, was founded by Mahabat Khan and the tomb is that of his son Lahrasp, who was given the title of Mahabat Khan after the death of his father. He (Lahrasp) was twice made governor of Kabul and died in AH1085 (1674 AD) while he was on his way from Kabul to Delhi.

The eastern half of the garden area has disappeared and modern buildings have been erected (by private persons) on it. The remaining portion is also in desolate state and under threat by the encroachers.

The monument lies in Baghbanpura towards the left of the road as one proceeds to Shalamar Garden from the city of Lahore. It now hardly presents the pristine glory

Wazir Khan's Mosque: General view from northeast.

10. Name of Monument: Wazir Khan's Mosque.

a) Owned and maintained by	Government (DAP)
b) Category/Classification	I
c) Character & Date/Period	Muslim, Religious/ AH 1044 (1634 AD)
d) Whether demarcated	Yes
e) Area	
f) Number & date of Notification:	No. 1403, dated 8.6.1925.

DESCRIPTION:

As recorded in the inscriptions, this exquisite mosque was founded in 1634 AD by Hakim Ilmud Din Ansari entitled Nawab Wazir Khan, native of Chiniot, District Jhang, and a Viceroy of Punjab under Emperor Shahjahan.

Wazir Khan's Mosque presents a unique phase of art of decoration in

Mughal architecture, namely, the variegated glazed tile and mosaic work, apparently introduced in this part of the country from Thatta in the 16th century AD. Such is the variety of designs, both in enamelled mosaic work and fresco paintings, that the Mosque in itself is a school of design. Cypress as a decorative design in enamelled mosaic work appears for the very first time in this Mosque.

Superb calligraphy in mosaic and the improved octagonal minarets, one of the earliest of this type in Mughal architecture, are its other distinctive features. It is rightly called the ornament of the city.

Like many other living mosques, it also had never been in the custody of the Department of Archaeology, Pakistan, since at least the time of the

Wazir Khan's Mosque: Prayer chamber and the niche.

inception of the Auqaf Department (1960) under the Provincial Government. As the state of the preservation of especially the rich embellishment was not satisfactory a comprehensive plan was chalked out and work on the restoration started in 1971 under the direction of Waliullah Khan. These operations continued till about 1984-85 resulting in almost the complete renovation, though on the original lines, of its decorative arts as also some structural conservation.

Wazir Khan's Mosque: The elegant corner Minar with exquisite embellishment.

Wazir Khan's Mosque: General view from the courtyard with the Tomb of Sayyid Muhammad Ishaq alias Miran Badshah.

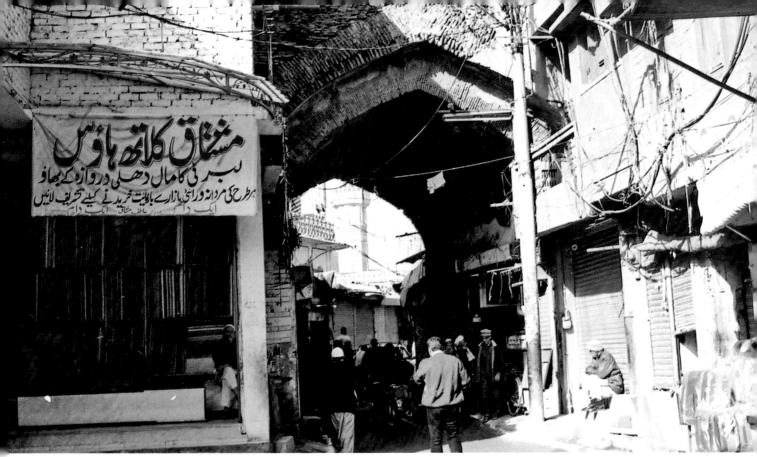

General view of Chitta Gate.

11. Name of Monument: **Chitta Gate (Chowk Wazir Khan inside Delhi Gate, Lahore).**

a) Owned and maintained by   Government (DAP)

b) Category/Classification   II

c) Character & Date/Period

d) Whether demarcated   Yes

e) Area   464-478'-6" x117'-6"

f) Number & date of Notification: No. F.4-20/159-EVT. Dated 29.4.1967

DESCRIPTION:

Chitta Gate is situated closely to the Wazir Khan Mosque on the eastern side. It appears that it was the entrance of the outer premises of the Wazir Khan Mosque. Since it is part of the Mosque planning, its date of construction is the same as that of the Mosque i.e. 1631 AD. The gate is about 16 feet wide and 30 feet high in shape of an arch. It is not in a good state of preservation while additionally heavily encroached upon by vendors. The monument is also in the possession and under the control of the Auqaf Department of the Government of Punjab.

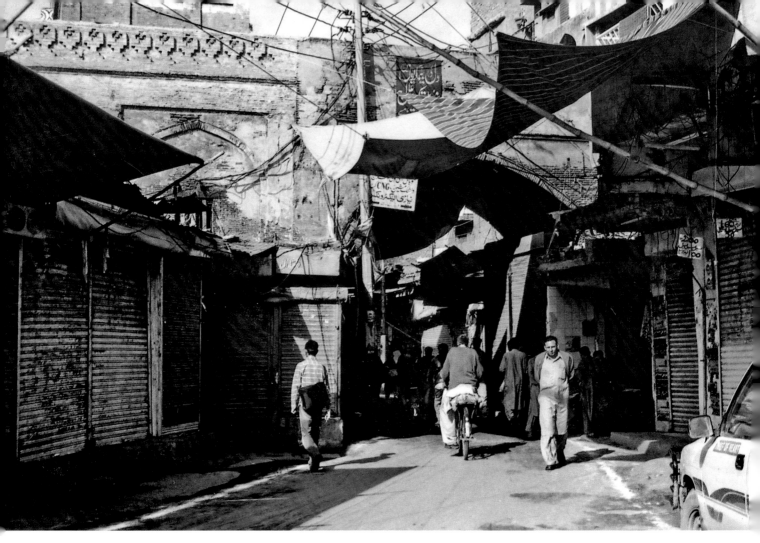

12. Name of Monument: Other Gate on NE of Wazir Khan Mosque (Chowk Wazir Khan, Lahore).

a) Owned and maintained by   Government (DAP)
b) Category/Classification   II
c) Character & Date/Period
d) Whether demarcated   Yes
e) Area   224 sft.
f) Number & date of Notification: No.F.4-20/59-EVT
                                  dated 29.4.1967.

DESCRIPTION:

It is high-arched Gateway and seems to be a part of the complex of Wazir Khan Mosque. As such its date of construction is the dame as that of the Mosque. Now this Gateway is also being used by the vendors etc. The Provincial Auqaf Department is responsible for its look after.

Wazir Khan's Hammam: View of the roof.

13.   Name of Monument: Wazir Khan's Hammam.

a) Owned and maintained by   Government (DAP)
b) Category/Classification   I
c) Character & Date/Period   Muslim, Secular/
                                 1634 AD
d) Whether demarcated   Yes
e) Area
f) Number & date of Notification: No. F.18-6/54-Estt,
                                     Dated 24.1.1955.

DESCRIPTION:

Wazir Khan's Hammam is situated inside Delhi Gate, near Chowk Wazir Khan. The complex was built by Sheikh Ilmud-din Ansari entitled Wazir Khan, a native of Chiot, who founded the splendid mosque known after his name lying not much away from this monument. The Hammam is surrounded by shops on its north, south and west, while on its eastern side is situated the Delhi Gate.

The Hammam is a single storey structure, of imposing extent, plan and proportion, covering a total area of 1,110 sft. It consists of only one structure of two blocks different in planning and separated by a passage.

Wazir Khan's Hammam: Interior view.

The monument is built of small sized bricks, as used in Mughal period buildings in the city of Lahore, with lime mixed with small pebbles and fragments of bricks as bonding material. The northern half of the western façade, including the main entrance, shows the original exterior of the Hammam. The exterior has indeed a character peculiarly of its own, for it is of cut and dressed bricks and with regular rectangular recessed panels. The parapet wall shows *zanjira* type continuous decoration in relief. The northeastern and northwestern angles of the building still retain the semi-octagonal *guldastas*. The Hammam has twelve domes and one semi-dome of the main entrance. The grouping of three small domes on each side of the high dome of the octagonal hall of the northern block is very effective. The dome of the octagonal hall of the northern block is a compounded type of dome as it is raised on a high drum pierced with windows.

The building complex of Hammam had been given by the Provincial Government for its utilization by the by the Lahore Municipal Corporation for a children school, dispensary and offices of the Health Department prior to the undertaking of a Restoration Project. The work was assigned to the Lahore Development Authority (LDA) – in the later half of the 1980s. Although services of a British Architect were also utilised yet the plan was prepared and executed without much input of any archaeologist or an archaeological conservation expert. The resultant work, though very pleasing to the eye, has given it a look of a new building, especially surface decorations, even if done generally keeping in view the original patterns. After the renovation it is being utilised as Tourist Information Centre.

Wazir Khan's Hammam: Interior view.

Wazir Khan's Baradari: Frontal view.

14. Name of Monument: Wazir Khan's Baradari

a) Owned and maintained by	Government (DAP)
b) Category/Classification	II
c) Character & Date/Period	Muslim, Secular/
	c. 1635 AD
d) Whether demarcated	
e) Area	16K-8M-121sft.
f) Number & date of Notification:	No. F.5/76-A.D.,
	Dated April,1976.

DESCRIPTION:

The square edifice known as Wazir Khan's *Baradari*, is a beautiful specimen of civic architecture going back to the period of Mughal Emperor Shahjahan. Built in about 1635 AD by Hakim Shaikh Ilmuddin Ansari, entitled Wazir Khan, a Minister and Governor of Punjab during the Emperor's. The existing building stands at the back of the Lahore Museum now isolated from its original garden environment. The *Baradari* has twelve arched openings, three on each side, and adorned with four corner cupolas. The main chamber is surrounded by four "*Pesh-Dalan*" (fore-courts) and was once crowned by a high dome, which has disappeared since long. The interior was originally decorated with fresco panelling done in multicolour, producing a pleasing effect in harmony with the picturesque surroundings of a spacious 'date garden" called "*Nakhliya*", which has since disappeared.

During the Sikh period, it became a part of their cantonment. It continued to serve as soldier's quarters during the British period till the cantonment was shifted to Mian Mir Area. It was then used as Settlement and Telegraph Office and later on, remained part of the Museum for sometime. It was also used to house a part of the Punjab

Wazir Khan's Baradari: SE site.

Public Library, which function it is still pressed into except for a period of few years during the early 1980s when it was handed over to the Department of Archaeology, Government of Pakistan for archaeological conservation and partial renovation.

Dai Anga's Mosque.

15. Name of Monument: Dai Anga's Mosque, Naulakha.

a) Owned and maintained by | Private
b) Category/Classification | II
c) Character & Date/Period | Muslim, Religious/
  | AH 1045 / 1635 AD
d) Whether demarcated | Yes
e) Area |
f) Number & date of Notification: | No. 47,
  | Dated 9.1.1913.

DESCRIPTION:

Situated near the Railway Station of Lahore and notable for its minute and refined enamelled tile mosaic wok, this mosque, as recorded in the inscription, was constructed in 1635 AD by Dai Anga, the wet nurse of Shahjahan's, whose real name was Zebun Nisa.

It is the only surviving monument of a decent quarter of Mughal period at Lahore called Mohalla Dai Anga, a locality of rich men and nobles of the city.

Ranjit Singh used the mosque as a military magazine. Later on, it was turned into a private residence of Mr. Henry Cone, an editor of the 'Lahore Chronicle', newspaper and press, who sold it subsequently to the Railway Company. It was restored in 1903 AD to Muslims to resume its function as a religious place.

Ranjit Singh used the mosque as a military magazine. Later on, it was turned into a private residence of Mr. Henry Cone, an editor of the 'Lahore Chronicle', newspaper and press, who sold it subsequently to the Railway Company

Jahangir's Mausoleum: General view from the Entrance Gate on west.

16. Name of Monument: Jahangir's Tomb and Compound

a) Owned and maintained by	Government (DAP)
b) Category/Classification	I
c) Character & Date/Period	Muslim, Religious/ 1637 AD
d) Whether demarcated	Yes
e) Area	41.7 Acres (398K-11M)
f) Number & date of Notification:	740, dated 4.12.1911.

DESCRIPTION:

The tomb of the Mughal Emperor Jahangir (1569-1627 AD) stands conspicuously amidst a luxuriant garden on the right bank of the river Ravi at Shahdara on the northwestern outskirts of Lahore. Jahangir died at

Rajauri on his way to Kashmir and was buried according to his will in this beautiful garden, which was called as 'Dilkusha' and belonged to his celebrated queen, Nur Jahan. The garden and the tomb complex are enclosed by a high brick-wall with an imposing gateway on the western side, which links it with the Akbari Sarai. The entire garden is *chahar-bagh* pattern and divided into sixteen squares by brick paved walkways with water channels in the middle and square or ornamental water tanks at each intersection.

The tomb is a single-storeyed square structure in plan, measuring 267 feet on each side and standing on a high platform. An arcaded veranda runs in front of the series of rooms and four vaulted bays lead to the central burial chamber, of which the western one provides access to the marble tombstone of the Emperor marking the grave underneath. The sarcophagus and the platform are richly inlaid with semi-precious stones depicting floral patterns and ninety-nine attributes of Allah. The entrance bay is profusely ornamented with fresco paintings on the ceiling and sidewalls in which the mosaic work at lower dado level enhances the beauty of the passage. Designs made of cut pieces of various stones such as *'sang-e-badal', 'sang-e-abri'*, black and white marble on the floor add to the aesthetic colour scheme of the lavish ornamentation. Four octagonal minarets on each corner of the square structure are built in four stages, which are

Jahangir died at Rajauri on his way to Kashmir and was buried according to his will in this beautiful garden, which was called as 'Dilkusha' and belonged to his celebrated queen, Nur Jahan

Jahangir's Mausoleum: Highly embellished western façade with Entrance to the sarcophagus Chamber.

Jahangir's Mausoleum: Southern side,
restoration operations in 1997.

Jahangir's Mausoleum: Architectural elements being prepared according
to original design to replace the worn out, damaged or missing portions.

crowned with cupolas. The three stages in the middle of the minarets are decorated with horizontally laid zigzag designs created by inlay of white, yellow and black marble. Each stage is defined by railing resting on marble brackets. The decorative designs of the tomb combine to create an overall effect of strength and gracefulness.

The original features of the roof have changed because of plundering of stones in the later period. It may have contained a pavilion of white marble but at present, a square platform with patchwork in different stones exists in the central part. The Sikhs reportedly removed the marble from the roof of the tomb for use in Golden Temple at Amritsar. This monument was also used

Jahangir's Mausoleum: Top burji of Main Entrance, speaks volumes of neglect.

as the residence of the French officer in the Sikh army. It was also given to Sultan Muhammad Khan, the brother of Dost Muhammad Khan of Afghanistan, who also caused considerable damage to it.

The entrance gate of the tomb is a monument in itself. It is a double storeyed structure, the exterior of which is decorated with inlaid geometric and floral design made in red sandstone panels. The half dome of the arch of the passageway shows honeycombed pendentives flanked by panels representing pinnacles and bunches of flowers.

Jahangir's Mausoleum: View of compound (garden) west of the mausoleum building.

17. Name of Monument: Akbari Sarai and Mosque

a) Owned and maintained by   Government (DAP)
b) Category/Classification   I
c) Character & Date/Period   Muslim, Religious/
                                  1637 AD
d) Whether demarcated   Yes
e) Area   9.14 Acres (88K-9M)
f) Number & date of Notification: No. 740, dated 4.12.1911

DESCRIPTION:

Jahangir's Tomb is approached through a spacious Sarai, which, contrary to what appears from its name, was not built by Akbar. Mullah Abdul Hamid, the court historian of Shahjahan, mentions the Sarai in his book 'Badshah Nama' under the name of *Jilau Khana-e-Rauza,* literally attached court of the Tomb. The open courtyard is flanked on all sides by raised terrace, on which are built rows of small cells, 180 in all, fronted with a veranda and a common open passage. The corners are occupied by *burjs*. It has got two stately gateways of usual Mughal style, one on the north and the other on the south.

From the structural evidence and the size of bricks, it appears that the Sarai and the entrance gateway of the tomb were built simultaneously and were integral parts of the same building project of Shahjahan's period. The Sarai was meant for the wayfarers and also to accommodate the establishment looking after the tomb. However, during the British period, towards the end of 19th century, it was used as the manufacturing depot of the North Western Railway.

An old mosque of the period of Shahjahan, though claiming no pretension, stands in the middle of the western wall, perhaps to provide *'jawab'* - literally answer - architectural balance, so important in the Mughal architecture.

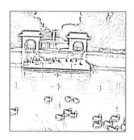

Mullah Abdul Hamid, the court historian of Shahjahan, mentions the Sarai in his book 'Badshah Nama' under the name of Jilau Khana-e-Rauza, literally attached court of the Tomb

Akbari Serai: General view looking west. The Mosque and part of the dome of Asif Khan's Tomb also visible.

Shalamar Gardens: View of second terrace showing a part of the water tank with fountains and recently constructed red sandstone pavilion to replace the Sikh period intervention.

18. Name of Monument:

Shalamar Garden, including Baradari, Gateway, Kiosks, pavilions, Bara Harta Well, Naqqar Khana, Asmani Well, and Garden.

a) Owned and maintained by   Government (DAP)
b) Category/Classification   I
c) Character & Date/Period   Muslim Secular/
Date of completion: AH 1052
(1642 AD)

Shalamar Gardens: Looking at the extent of second and third terraces from the first terrace pavilion.

d) Whether demarcated	Yes
e) Area	41.65 Acres (403k-4m)
f) Number & date of Notification:	47 Dated: 9.1.1913

DESCRIPTION:

Terraced and walled gardens with pavilions and canals running through the centre were another innovation introduced, for the very first time, in the architectural and landscape history of the sub-continent, by Mughal Emperor Shahjahan. These gardens are well known to the world by their popular name of 'Shalamar'.

The Garden: This garden occupies some 40 acres of land and was laid in 1642 AD, at the command of Emperor Shahjahan after the plan of the Royal Gardens in Kashmir and was completed at a cost of Rs. Six lakhs under the superintendence of Khallilullah Khan. Shah Nahar, later known as Hansli Canal, was brought to irrigate the garden from Rajpur, present Madhupur, at a distance of more than a hundred miles, costing two lakhs of rupees.

Shalamar Gardens: First terrace pavilion seemingly a later replacement of the original Mughal period one. Also seen are the Aabshar – Cascade – and the white marble Takht or Throne.

Shalamar Gardens: Walkways and water arrangement of the 1st Terrace. At far back is the Pavilion overlooking the 2nd Terrace.

The uppermost terrace of the garden is called 'Farah Bakhsh' (pleasure-giving), and the middle and lower most terraces combined are named as 'Faiz Bakhsh' (bountiful). However, it may be noted that the Emperor, or any one in his period, ever called it by the famous name it now carries universally.

The Buildings: The garden was laid out as a royal recreation place as well as for providing accommodation whenever the Emperor was on a visit to Lahore. For this purpose a number of pavilions and summerhouses were constructed in it. In the upper-most terrace, the present main entrance was originally the *aramgah* (rest room) of the Emperor, Shahjahan.

The building (rather a complex of buildings) on the east in the same terrace, now known as *Naqqar Khana*, was *Jharoka-e-Daulat Khana-e-khas-o-am* (the window of the hall of Special and Common Audience), and that on the west was the residence of the Empress. In the middle terrace, there is a hammam on the east, which was originally decorated with pietra dura work. Besides, there are six corner *burjis* surmounted by domes and four pavilions in the second and one in the third terrace.

The garden suffered much during turbulent times of Ahmed Shah Abdali (1747 –1772 AD) and the Sikhs, who robbed almost all of its decorative works in marble, red sandstone and pietra dura for re-using the same in their own buildings elsewhere.

The garden suffered much during turbulent times of Ahmed Shah Abdali (1747 –1772 AD) and the Sikhs, who robbed almost all of its decorative works in marble, red sandstone and pietra dura for re-using the same in their own buildings elsewhere

Tomb of Asif Khan: Main Gateway on the south.

During the reign of Ranjit Singh it was stripped off of all its marble facing of the dome and interior leaving only the damaged marble cenotaph, which is inlaid with pietra dura in floral patterns with ninety-nine attributes of God in Naskh calligraphy

19. Name of Monument: Tomb of Asif Khan and Compound

a) Owned and maintained by	Government (DAP)
b) Category/Classification	I
c) Character & Date/Period	Muslim, Religious/ 1645 AD.
d) Whether demarcated	Yes
e) Area	1.2 Acres
f) Number & date of Notification:	No.740, dated 4.12.1911.

DESCRIPTION:

Mirza Abul Hasan titled Asif Khan was the brother of Empress Nur Jahan and father of Arjumand Banu Begum, the celebrated consort of Emperor Shahjahan called in history as the lady of the Taj at Agra. In the 8th year of Shahjahan's reign he was made Khan-e-Khanan and Commander-in-Chief and a year later Governor of Lahore. He was a man of fabulous wealth and constructed his palace at Lahore at a cost of twenty lakhs. Asif Khan died in 1641 AD and his tomb was erected by Shahjahan. It took four years to build it and was completed at a cost of three lakhs of rupees.

Tomb of Asif Khan: A perfect picture of apathy and neglect – encroachments too close on the outer side (far background) and compound left unattended.

The tomb, an octagonal structure with a high bulbous dome, stands on an eight-sided podium originally of red sandstone in the midst of a spacious garden, which was once set with reservoirs, fountains and beautiful walkways. The entire area is enclosed by a brick-wall finished with lime plaster and is approached through an imposing gate on the south.

During the reign of Ranjit Singh it was stripped off of all its marble facing of the dome and interior leaving only the damaged marble cenotaph, which is inlaid with *pietra dura* in floral patterns with ninety-nine attributes of God in *Naskh* calligraphy. Originally the floor of the tomb was in mosaic of various stones, the inner dado in white marble, outer in *sang-e-abri* and the façade mostly in marble with a sprinkling of *sang-e-abri* and other variegated stones. An excellently done enamelled mosaic and tile-work, the traces of which are still extant, greatly enhanced the effect of the decoration in the interior of the building.

Tomb of Asif Khan: General view, giving ample evidence of its ruthless treatment at the hands of the Sikhs during their sway in Punjab.

Tomb of Nur Jahan: General view from northwest.

20. Name of Monument: Tomb of Nur Jahan

a) Owned and maintained by	Government (DAP)
b) Category/Classification	I
c) Character & Date/Period	Muslim, Religious/ 1645 AD
d) Whether demarcated	Yes
e) Area	9.06 Acres (87K)
f) Number & date of Notification:	No. 740, dated 4.12.1911

DESCRIPTION:

Nur Jahan, whose real name was Mehrun Nisa Begum, was the daughter of Mirza Ghiyas Baig entitled I'tamadud Daula, the prime minister of Emperor

Jahangir. She was first married to Ali Quli Baig surnamed Sher Afgan Khan, a *jagirdar* (big landlord) at Burdwan in Bengal, and later, in 1611 AD, to Jahangir and became his Empress sharing all responsibilities in the administration of the Empire. She was given the title of Nur Jahan (light of the world), and to show her share in the sovereignty, a gold coin was struck conjointly in her and the Emperor's name. She is also mentioned under the title of "Nur Mahal" (light of the palace). Having survived Jahangir by 18 years, she died in 1645 AD, and was buried in this mausoleum, which she herself built during her lifetime.

Tomb of Nur Jahan seen with a passing train on the track for which its continuity with other tombs in the complex was severed during the British period.

Standing on a platform 158 feet square, the tomb measures 134 feet square and standing 19 feet and 6 inches in height. The interior was originally finished with glazed lime plaster bearing beautiful floral fresco paintings, traces of which still exist here and there. The minute paintings done in difficult positions in the honeycombed cornices of some of the rooms are of special interest.

The present rough brick floor dates back to the Sikh period. It is presumed that the original floor was that of marble. The cut-brick floor of the outer platform was laid according to the original pattern by the Pakistan Department of Archaeology during the early 1960s.

The original cenotaph over the graves of Nur Jahan and her daughter Ladli Begum, the only other grave in the tomb, which are said to have been of marble, have also disappeared – the existing ones being laid later. The present marble platform was built by Hakim Ajmal Khan of Delhi in 1912 AD, who also put up the inscription giving the chronogram relating the date of her death.

A rose-garden, set up here to pay tributes to the genius of Nur Jahan, who had invented the rosewater, once did give it immense fame but even that has lost much of attraction, thanks to the apathetic attitude of the authorities

The Tomb of Nur Jahan with its vast garden originally made a part of the ensemble of the Tombs of Asif Khan and Jahangir but the laying of the Lahore-Rawalpindi rail track had cut it from the other two in the early 20th century. The truncated garden is now limited to the rail-track running on its eastern side, while the condition of the rest of it is also not enviable with much of it having been neglected over extended period of time. A rose-garden, set up here to pay tributes to the genius of Nur Jahan, who had invented the rosewater, once did give it immense fame but even that has lost much of attraction, thanks to the apathetic attitude of the authorities.

Chauburji (four-minaretted) remained Sehburji (three-minaretted) for a long time after it had lost the northwestern corner.

21.   Name of Monument: Chauburji (Mozang)

a) Owned and maintained by   Government (DAP)
b) Category/Classification   I
c) Character & Date/Period   Muslim Secular/AH 1056 (1646 AD)
d) Whether demarcated   Yes
e) Area   0.16 Acres
f) Number & date of Notification: 47/ dated 9.1.1913

DESCRIPTION:

Situated on the Multan Road, the monument was actually a gateway to a garden that has now disappeared. It is called Chauburji (the four minarets)

Chauburji after restoration of the fourth minaret.

because of its four corner minarets, out of which one on the northwestern corner was actually lost and it stood with three minarets for a long time. The fragmentary inscription on its eastern archway records that the garden was founded in 1646 AD by a lady mentioned metaphorically as "*Sahib-e-Zebinda, Begum-e-Dauran*" (one endowed with elegance, the lady of the age) and was bestowed upon one Mian Bai.

The reference is most probably to Jahan Ara Begum, the eldest daughter of Emperor Shahjahan, who was entitled "Lady of the age" after the death of her mother in 1631. That there was a garden of Jahan Ara Begum at Lahore is confirmed by two letters of Emperor Aurangzeb addressed to her.

The local tradition connects Zebinda with Zebunnissa Begum, the accomplished daughter of Aurangzeb and Mian Bai as her maidservant. This tradition, however, is incorrect, since Zebun Nisa, born in 1639, was still a child when the garden was founded.

Mian Bai is not known to history, but that she was a maid-servant is not supported by the fragmentary inscription on the southwest corner of the gateway, which records that the garden was constructed by Mian Bai, the pride of women (*Fakhrun Nisa*). From the word "Fakharun Nisa" it seems that she was a lady of some status.

The main architectural merit of the building is its rich mosaic decoration with which its entire façade, including the octagonal corner minarets, are brilliantly embellished. The minarets are slender for their height and end at the top in covered platforms, which once carried arched pavilions.

The panel over the main vault is inscribed with *Ayat-al-Kursi*, a verse of the Holy Quran, in blue enamelled letters. At the end of this inscription, the year AH 1056 (corresponding to 1646) is also given.

From the original Chauburji (four minarets) it had become sehburji (three minarets) because of the falling to ground the whole of one corner with one minaret probably during the British period. It continued to stand like that till the Department of Archaeology, Pakistan undertook a plan to restore the monument in its original shape. The work was started in 1973, raising the

Chauburji: A drawing made out in 1854 captioned as "Ruins of a Gateway on the Road to Multan".

fourth – northwestern – minaret right from its old foundations. The project, with certain hiccups due to the involvement of other agencies, was completed in 1979. Later on, to save it from the fast coming up encroachments and to give it a central place as a remarkable landmark, it area was turned into a traffic island at the confluence of Multan Road, Bahawalpur Road, Lake Road, Lower Mall and a couple of smaller roads connecting it to other quarters. Another conservation/preservation operation was carried out during 1996-97 when some of the undermined walls were underpinned and worn out brick-tiles of the structure replaced to give it a further lease of life.

It is called Chauburji (the four minarets) because of its four corner minarets, out of which one on the northwestern corner was actually lost and it stood with three minarets for a long time

Gulabi Bagh Gateway: General view.

22. Name of Monument: Gulabi Bagh Gateway.

a) Owned and maintained by   Government (DAP)

b) Category/Classification   I

c) Character & Date/Period   Muslim Secular/AH 1066 (1655 AD)

d) Whether demarcated   Yes

e) Area   0.20 Acres (1k-10m)

f) Number & date of Notification: No. 47/ dated: 9.1.1913.

DESCRIPTION:

Notable for its excellence of rich and vivid mosaic tile work and superb calligraphy on plaster base, this was the entrance gate to a pleasure garden, which, like so many others at Lahore, has now disappeared. It was constructed by a Persian noble, Mirza Sultan Baig, who was *Amirul Bahr* (Admiral of Fleet). It is said that in 1657 AD while on a hunting excursion to the royal hunting reserve at Hiran Minar near Sheikhupura, he died from the bursting of an English gun given to him by Emperor Shahjahan. The title "Gulabi Bagh" (Rose Garden) occurs in the last line of the inscription over the archway, which not only describes the kind of the garden, but as a chronogram also gives the date of its construction in Hijra era, which corresponds to 1655 AD.

With the ugly encroachments coming too close to the superb piece of the art of the architectural embellishment, it is now hard to visualise its original grandeur.

Closer look at highly embellished panels.

Buddhu's Tomb; General view.

23. Name of Monument: Buddhu's Tomb (so-called).

a) Owned and maintained by   Government (DAP)

b) Category/Classification   I

c) Character & Date/Period   Muslim, Secular
1671 AD

d) Whether demarcated   Yes

e) Area   0.12 Acres (1k-4m)

f) Number & date of Notification: No. 1730,
Dated: 22.11.1912.

DESCRIPTION:

Buddhu was a brick manufacturer during the time of Emperor Shahjahan. The tomb situated on the right side of Grand Trunk (GT) Road near Gulabi Bagh Gateway is a simple brick structure. It has one arched opening on

Site of Buddhu's Awa (brick-kiln). Also seen in the background on left is the Tomb.

Buddhu was a brick manufacturer during the time of Emperor Shahjahan. The tomb situated on the right side of Grand Trunk (GT) Road near Gulabi Bagh Gateway is a simple brick structure

each side and is surmounted by a low-pitched dome, carried on a high cylindrical drum over an octagonal base. The exterior of the building is panelled and finished with plaster. The dome, carried on squinches, is decorated with enamelled tiles in blue, yellow, white, green and light chocolate colours laid in zigzag pattern. Although the monument is called Buddhu's Tomb, it is in all probability, the tomb of Faqir Abdul Haque, a saint who died in 1671 AD.

The site of the Buddhu's Awa (brick-kiln) is also situated nearby and marked by a small pillar. However, the whole area has now turned into the den of vehicles workshops, which carry on their business right in the protected premises quite unabated and unchecked.

Dai Anga's Tomb, general view.

24. Name of Monument: Dai Anga's Tomb

a) Owned and maintained by	Government (DAP)
b) Category/Classification	I
c) Character & Date/Period	Muslim Secular/ AH 1082 (1671 AD)
d) Whether demarcated	Yes
e) Area	(Not mentioned)
f) Number & Date of Notification:	No. 47 Dated: 9.1.1913

DESCRIPTION:

Behind the Gulabi Bagh Gateway and on the site of the former garden lies the mausoleum of Dai Anga, wet-nurse of Emperor Shahjahan. She was the wife of Murad Khan, a Mughal Magistrate of Bikaner. She was the founder of Dai Anga's Mosque, one of the well-known ancient mosques of Lahore. (given above at S.No.14) The Quranic inscription on the walls of the tomb chamber ends in the name of the scribe, Muhammad Salih, and the date AH1082 (1671 AD)., which seems to be the year when the tomb was constructed. Brick-built and square in plan, the tomb stands on a low platform under which lie the actual burials in a subterranean chamber. The mausoleum comprising of a central tomb chamber and eight rooms around it, was once beautifully decorated with mosaic work. The roof bears a low-pitched dome on a high neck and a square kiosk in each corner supported on slender brick pillars. The original two cenotaphs have been replaced later by the existing brick-built ones.

Tomb of Nawab Bahadur Khan: General view.

25. Name of Monument: Tomb of Nawab Bahadur Khan

a) Owned and maintained by   Government (DAP)
b) Category/Classification   I
c) Character & Date/Period   Muslim, Religious/ About 1678 AD
d) Whether demarcated   No
e) Area   13,280 Sft.
f) Number & date of Notification: No. F.5-9/57-Estt,
                                Dated: 17.3.1958.

DESCRIPTION:

Nawab Bahadur Khan died in 1678 AD and the tomb must have been constructed about the same time. The Mausoleum, octagonal in plan with high arches on each side, stands on an octagonal platform, which was exposed lately after removing the debris and rubbish lying over it. The entire building is constructed in cut brickwork without any use of red sandstone, which is a significant point. Its exterior is decorated with panelling in the form of *zanjira* and niches, which represents another unique architectural feature. The dome is low-pitched. In the early British period the tomb was used as theatre hall. Now it stands almost neglected portraying the state of complacence of the authorities.

Badshahi Mosque: General view of the courtyard, ablution tank and prayer chambers as seen from the upper arch of the Entrance Gate. Photograph: c. mid-1960s.

26. Name of Monument: Badshahi Mosque.

a) Owned and maintained by   Government (DAP)

b) Category/Classification   I

c) Character & Date/Period   Muslim, Religious/
    AH 1084 (1673-74 AD)

d) Whether demarcated   Yes

e) Area

f) Number & date of Notification: No. 1403, dated 8.6.1925.

DESCRIPTION:

Badshahi (Imperial) Mosque at Lahore, which is also sometimes called as Alamgiri Masjid, was built during the period of Emperor Aurangzeb Alamgir in the year 1673-74 AD. Measuring 576 square feet in plan the mosque is built on a raised platform. The main entrance – in itself a monument of merit

– is on the east, which is approached by a flight of 22 steps rising from three sides and ending on the red sandstone platform. The vast courtyard measuring about 530 square feet is divided into two parts: the upper and the lower. This latter part is called *fina* where funeral prayers can also be offered. It is also in this part that the ablution tank is laid, though it is not used for this purpose now. The tank is 50 feet square in plan and about 3 feet deep. Its sidewalls were originally lined with *sang-e-abri* slabs.

The upper part is further divided into three parts: the central portion or the main courtyard of the mosque proper and the two side ones, which are lower by one step than the central one.

The courtyard is flanked all around by *hujras* (cells), 80 in number, which served as a pert of *madrassa* (seminary) in Mughal days. *Hujras* on the east were pulled down by the British in 1856, to forestall the use of the Grand Mosque as a fort against the foreign rulers. However, after its restitution to the Muslims, wall has been reconstructed here but converting the place in to long arcaded ablution halls.

The interior consists of two deep and long halls. The front compartment is divided in to two big halls by the intercepting central vault. The back portion is divided in to seven intercommunicated halls or bays by means of eight thick arches on massive jambs, which were a technical necessity to take the load of the heavy roof and domes above. The dado of the whole

Badshahi (Imperial) Mosque at Lahore, which is also sometimes called as Alamgiri Masjid, was built during the period of Emperor Aurangzeb Alamgir in the year 1673-74 AD. Measuring 576 square feet in plan the mosque is built on a raised platform

A panoramic view from Fort's Haveli of Mai Jindan. In addition to Badshahi Mosque, Makatib Khana, Moti Masjid and Ranjit Singh's Smadh are also visible.

Badshahi Mosque: Cells being provided with red sandstone face thought by the Punjab Auqaf Department Committee being the original material. Photograph: 1997.

of the interior is of well-polished *sang-e-abri*. The rest of the interior with the exception of the *mehrab*, niche, and spandrels of the central hall, which have marble veneer, is finished with lime plaster bearing in relief a floral network of excellent workmanship, attractive in shape and the curves suited to different positions. Though it is tastefully painted with bright colours in fresco yet the overall effect is that of a sober composition.

On the top or the skyline of the prayer chamber, four corner octagonal minarets, four *guldastas*, two in front flanking the central vault and

Badshahi Mosque: Interior view.

Badshahi Mosque: The imposing Gateway, in itself a monument.

two on the back in response and three beautiful bulbous domes with a superb refined curvature constructed at the neck, greatly add to its architectural accomplishment. The central dome with a diameter of 63 feet is bigger than the rest. The minarets and *guldastas*, in order to break the monotony, are all in-laid in white marble vertical lines and surmounted with pavilions crowned with beautiful cupolas in white marble with beautiful glittering gilded pinnacles of copper.

The four corner *minars* with an outer circumference of 67 feet rise 176 feet high above their plinth. The top pavilion carried over 8 octagonal columns is alone 32 feet high, circular and hollow inside the centre, is occupied by a vertical shaft round which run 204 steps to ascend to the top pavilion, which gives a bird's eye view of Lahore.

A general view of Hazuri Bagh with Sikh Baradari in the middle. Also seen in the background is the Alamgiri Gate of the Fort.

27. Name of Monument: Hazuri Bagh and Baradari

a) Owned and maintained by	Government (DAP)
b) Category/Classification	I
c) Character & Date/Period	Muslim & Sikh Secular,
	Marble Baradari & Garden 1818 AD
	AH 1084 (1673-74 AD)
d) Whether demarcated	Yes
e) Area	2.3 Acres (22k-19m)
f) Number & date of Notification:	No. 11078, dated: 9.4.1924
	No. 47 dated: 9.1.1913

DESCRIPTION:

The quadrangle now occupied by the garden called Hazuri Bagh with a marble *Baradari* (1818 AD) in its centre, was originally a serai built by Aurangzeb, where during the Mughal rule thronged the Imperial cavalcades and armed retainers.

The two-storeyed building adjoining the southern gateway (Hazuri Bagh Gate) was also originally built in the time of Aurangzeb as a boarding house for scholars. Later on it was used as *Abdar-Khana* or place for keeping refreshing drinks. During the reign of Ranjit Singh it came to be called *Gulabkhana* or "Rose-water House", literally rose-house. During the British period it was again used as a boarding house for students.

The Marble *Baradari* was constructed in 1818 AD by Ranjit Singh from materials obtained by despoiling the Mughal buildings in Lahore, specially the tomb of Nawankot and Shah Sharaf's tomb which once stood near Bhati Gate. It appears that the marble floor of the Royal Bath in the Lahore Fort was also removed for this purpose as evidence may still be seen on the eastern side of the platform of the *Baradari*.

Here it was that the Sikh Maharaja used to sit in state and transact

Hazuri Bagh, looking towards Alamgiri Gate.

business of his kingdom, and it was also in this *baradari* that Sher Singh received the British Embassy sent by Lord Ellenborough in 1843 AD.

This building, measuring 45 feet 6 inches square, was originally two-storeyed structure. Built entirely in white marble it also has underground chambers. Its upper storey was struck by lightening in 1932 and collapsed leaving it with a look of a single-storey edifice. The original ceiling, with stucco tracery inlaid with convex mirrors is also a typical architectural decorative feature seen especially in Sikh period buildings. Though built of despoiled materials, it nevertheless gives a pleasing look and has no mean merit in building art.

On the northern side of the Hazuri Bagh is situated the Roshnai Darwaza (Gate), which gave access to this area and then onward to the city of Lahore. As already mentioned elsewhere, it was this portal through which the nobles passed on their way to the palace. It used to be illuminated profusely after dark, which earned it the name of Roshnai Darwaza or the Gate of the Lights. It was here under this entrance that Prince Nau Nihal Singh, son of Maharaja Kharak Singh and Mian Udham Singh, eldest son of Gulab Singh, were fatally wounded by the fall of a portion of an archway as they were returning after the cremation of Maharaja Kharak Singh's mortal remains.

The cells on both sides of the Roshnai Gate have now been turned into the residences of the officers of the Department of Archaeology, Pakistan, while those in the southern boundary wall of the Hazuri Bagh serve as premises for the Ulema Academy, under the charge of the Punjab Auqaf Department. The Garden itself has turned into a cultural spot where, especially on holidays, groups of people sit in the plots to listen to the rendering of the famous folk songs or the Punjabi classics like Heer Waris Shah or Saiful Maluk of Mian Muhammad Bakhsh.

It used to be illuminated profusely after dark, which earned it the name of Roshnai Darwaza or the Gate of the Lights. It was here under this entrance that Prince Nau Nihal Singh, son of Maharaja Kharak Singh and Mian Udham Singh, eldest son of Gulab Singh, were fatally wounded by the fall of a portion of an archway as they were returning after the cremation of Maharaja Kharak Singh's mortal remains

Hazuri Bagh with Baradari in the centre. Roshnai Gate is behind it while dome of Ranjit Singh's Smadh is visible towards far left.

Kos Minar in Garhi Shahu.

28. Name of Monument: One Kos Minar (Garhi Shahu) and Two Kos Minars (Minola near Jullo).

a) Owned and maintained by   Government (DAP)
b) Category/Classification   II
c) Character & Date/Period   Muslim Secular/
     17th Century AD
d) Whether demarcated   Yes
e) Area   Less than One Marla
f) Number & date of Notification: No. 24847
     Dated: 17.10.1921

In 1609 Emperor Jahangir ordered a small minaret-like monument to be built at every Kos along the Grand Trunk Road. The Kos was an ancient measure of the territory distance, which varied from time to time

DESCRIPTION:

The Muslim Emperors of South Asia Subcontinent took good care of the major roadways leading to different regions. One of the principal highways of the country was the 'Sarak-e-Azam' or the Grand Trunk Road as known by the later British. It connected the middle Gangetic plains with the Mountain Pass to Kabul. It served as a major backbone of communication in earlier days. It was the main channel of international and inter-regional travel. A part of it was repeatedly traversed by the grand Mughals and their retinues on their periodical excursions to Kashmir or eastern areas of the empire.

In 1609 Emperor Jahangir ordered a small minaret-like monument to be built at every *Kos* along the Grand Trunk Road. The *Kos* was an ancient measure of the territory distance, which varied from time to time. It is believed to have been derived from the word *Krosa* meaning a "cry" used as an indication of distance as early as 300 BC. It was probably known also to Hieun Tsang in the seventh century AD. During the period of Emperor Jahangir the conventional Kos measured between 2 miles 3 furlongs to 2 miles 5 furlongs.

Although most of such 'milestones' have perished with time there were still 4 of such Kos Minars of Mughal period exist in the environs of Lahore. One of them, and perhaps in a better state of preservation, is the one in the Garhi Shahu area, near the main railway line. It is built of burnt bricks about 27 feet high, with an octagonal base and cone-shaped super structure but is without any inscription.

One of the other Kos Minars, situated about six miles from Jallo, is also in somewhat recognisable shape while the rest have either perished or are in the advanced stage of decay and deterioration. But without any exception, they more on the mercy of the nature and general man and in no way being looked after by the authorities as protected antiquity.

Kos Minar near Jallo.

Tomb of Ali Mardan.

29. Name of Monument: Tomb of Ali Mardan and Gateway:

a) Owned and maintained by	Government (DAP)
b) Category/Classification	I
c) Character & Date/Period	Muslim Religious
	17th Century AD
d) Whether demarcated	Yes
e) Area	1.9 Acres (11 kanals – 9 marlas)
f) Name & date of Notification:	No. 149
	Dated: 5.2.1919

DESCRIPTION:

Ali Mardan Khan was the Governor of Qandahar under Shah Safi (1629 – 1642 AD) of Iran. Disgusted with the tyranny of the Shah, he surrendered Qandahar to Shahjahan in 1637 AD and took refuge in his court. He was appointed Governor of Kashmir and in 1639 AD Punjab was also given under his charge. In 1642 AD he received the high title of *Amirul Omara*, and was such a favourite of Shahjahan that the Emperor called him "*Yarwafadar*" (the faithful friend). He showed great skill and judgement in the execution of public works, especially canals. Among other works to his credit is the well-famed Shah Nahar of Shalamar Garden.

He died at Machhiwara on his way to Kashmir in 1656-57 AD, and was buried by the side of his mother in her tomb, which once stood in the midst of a garden. The Garden unfortunately has now totally disappeared with the exception of the gateway, which alone can give an idea of the excellence of enamelled tile mosaic work and its refined patterns, with which the entire monument was once decorated.

The tomb, a massive brick construction, octagonal in plan with a high dome and kiosks on angular points, stands on an eight-sided podium, each side measuring 57'-6". It was originally built with all the architectural grace typical of that time, but was vandalised by the Sikhs, who deprived the building of all its stone facing and other decorations, leaving only traces here and there. From the small pieces still intact, it appears that the dome was finished with white marble inlaid with floral designs in black marble.

Emperor called him "Yarwafadar" (the faithful friend). He showed great skill and judgement in the execution of public works, especially canals. Among other works to his credit is the well-famed Shah Nahar of Shalamar Garden

The state of preservation of the monument is no different from that of the others in the vicinity.

Gateway to Tomb of Ali Mardan.

Zebun-Nisa Tomb: General view.

30. Name of Monument: Tomb of (erroneously called) Zebun Nisa

a) Owned and maintained by   Government (DAP)

b) Category/Classification   I

c) Character & Date/Period   Muslim, Religious/
17th century AD

d) Whether demarcated   No

e) Area

f) Number & date of Notification: No. F.23-18/49-Estt,
dated: 30.11.1949.

DESCRIPTION:

About 270 feet west of the Gateway at Nawankot lies the stripped brick core of the undated tomb containing two unknown graves one perhaps of Zebun Nisa. A portion of the original tessellated floor having Shahjahani touch and delicacy and in which white and black marble and *sang-e-badal* (variegated stone) form the patterns, have survived the vandalism of the Sikhs, who stripped the tomb of its ornamentations and stone facing. The existing patches *of sang-e-badal* flooring are exactly similar to that of the veranda in Jahangir's Tomb. Its pyramidal dome, curvilinear externally and hemispherical internally, is the only example of its class at Lahore.

The monument is badly encroached upon on almost all of its sides. Even inside the Entrance, which ironically is provided with iron-grated gateway, there are running businesses of the sorts and hardly leave a good impression of the maintenance of the edifice.

The existing patches of sang-e-badal flooring are exactly similar to that of the veranda in Jahangir's Tomb. Its pyramidal dome, curvilinear externally and hemispherical internally, is the only example of its class at Lahore

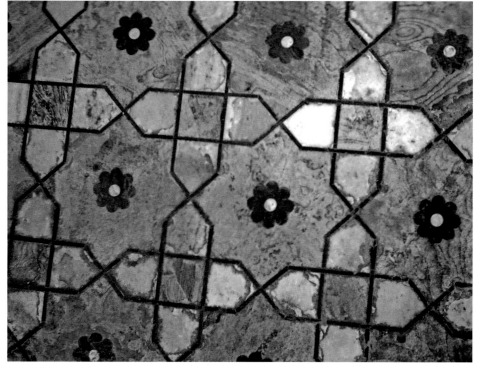

Zebun-Nisa Tomb: Pattern of variegated stone floor.

31. Name of Monument: Tiled Gateway and Two Bastions

a) Owned and maintained by	Government (DAP)
b) Category/Classification	I
c) Character & Date/Period	Muslim Secular/ 3rd part of 17th century AD.
d) Whether demarcated	Yes
e) Area	0.02 Acres (2K)
f) Number & date of Notification:	No. 943/ dated: 20.10.1914.

The tiled gateway and the corner towers were the entrance gate to a garden associated with Zaibun Nisa Begum. It is situated in the Nawankot area on the east of Multan Road, a mile south of Chauburji

DESCRIPTION:

The tiled gateway and the corner towers were the entrance gate to a garden associated with Zaibun Nisa Begum. It is situated in the Nawankot area on the east of Multan Road, a mile south of Chauburji.

The gateway is of usual Mughal design with a high central arch flanked with similar arched openings, two in the basement and two above. The note-worthy feature is the domed pavilion or kiosk, square in plan each side of which measures 6'-10", on each corner of the gateway. These pavilions are supported on brick-built square pillars, four on each side similar in shape as in Dai Anga's tomb. The domes of these pavilions are fluted and covered with glazed tiles. The upper stage on each side of the passage has terracotta *jalies* (screens) with network and zigzag patterns.

The gateway 43'-3" x 36'-9" and 30'-2" high is decorated with faience enamelled mosaic tiles in green, blue, yellow and orange laid in framed panels. The interior is richly embellished with fresco paintings in floral designs such as tendrils, flower vases and cypress in rich colour scheme where red and green predominate.

The corner towers are octagonal on plan with one arched opening in the basement. These are surmounted by octagonal domed pavilions with eight formed in golden yellow enamelled terracotta tiles separated with thin lines of green colour. The distance between the two towers, once forming the northeast and southeast corner of the disappeared garden, is 600 feet, which easily gives an idea of the extent of the erstwhile garden.

The antiquity here also stands encroached upon so mercilessly that one can hardly have a good view of it to appreciate its grandeur.

Tiled gateway or Nawankot Gateway.

Tomb of Khwaja Sabir.

32. Name of Monument: Tomb of Khwaja Sabir (Nawab Nusrat Khan)

a) Owned and maintained by   Government (DAP)

b) Category/Classification   II

c) Character & Date/Period   Muslim, Religious/
17th Century AD.

d) Whether demarcated   No

e) Area

f) Number & date of Notification: No. F.5-9/57-Estt.,
Dated 17.3.1958.

DESCRIPTION:

Nawab Nusrat Khan received the title of Khan-e-Dauran from Emperor Shahjahan. He died in Lahore in AH1070/1659 AD and his tomb was constructed during the rule of Aurangzeb.

This tomb lies between the tombs of Ali Mardan Khan and of Bahadur Khan, and is exactly the same in design and proportions as that of Bahadur Khan and belongs to the same period. The interior of the tomb is now used as a mosque but in the time of Ranjit Singh it was used as a private residence by Gen. Court, the same man who excavated around Mankiala Tope (Rawalpindi district). This General added some rooms, which, however, have now disappeared except the three arches in the upper storey on the west.

This is another monument under the control of the Government, which presents a pathetic state of neglect. The structure is fast deteriorating with plaster and decorations gone off from most of the surface. The walls are getting undermined and show clear signs of seepage.

In the time of Ranjit Singh it was used as a private residence by Gen. Court, the same man who excavated around Mankiala Tope (Rawalpindi district). This General added some rooms, which, however, have now disappeared except the three arches in the upper storey on the west

These are two gardens out of many, which were constructed subsequent to the building of Shalamar by Emperor Shahjahan in 1642 AD

Remnants of Inayat Bagh right within a residential quarter.

33. Name of Monument: Inayat, and Angoori Bagh opposite Shalamar Gardens.

a) Owned and maintained by   Private
b) Category/Classification   II
c) Character & Date/Period   Muslim, Secular/
                                        Middle of 17th century AD

d) Whether demarcated	Yes
e) Area	172K-13M
f) Number & date of Notification:	No. F.17-47/55-Estt, Dated 24.10.1955.

DESCRIPTION:

These are two gardens out of many, which were constructed subsequent to the building of Shalamar by Emperor Shahjahan in 1642 AD.

Nothing is left in Inayat Bagh or Angoori Bagh except broken structures of walls at certain points. Traces of two burjs of Inayat Bagh, one on the northwest corner and the other on the southeast corner, are perhaps the only visible signs of its past glory. Even these signs have now been amalgamated into the modern residence, and their amelioration in due time would not be noticed. The most ironical part in the destruction of these heritage features is the apathetic and callous approach of the Provincial government, which has 'developed' the area with the residential schemes known as Angoori Bagh Housing Scheme. So the systematic but irretrievable intervention has caused the loss, for all times to come, of some gems of past glory.

The most ironical part in the destruction of these heritage features is the apathetic and callous approach of the Provincial government, which has 'developed' the area with the residential schemes known as Angoori Bagh Housing Scheme

Remnants of Anguri Bagh encroached upon by modern buildings.

Tomb of Nadira Begam: General view.

34. Name of Monument: Nadira Begum's Tomb and Tank.

a) Owned and maintained by   Government (DAP)
b) Category/Classification   I
c) Character & Date/Period   Muslim, Religious/
                                    Second half of 17th century AD.
d) Whether demarcated   No
e) Area   537' x 533'
f) Number & date of Notification: No. F.17-107/55-Estt.
                                    dated: 27.8.1956.

DESCRIPTION:

Nadira Begum, wife of the unfortunate Prince Dara Shikoh, died of dysentery during his wandering in Sindh at the time of the war of succession to the throne between him and Aurangzeb, his younger brother. She died in about 1659 AD and her body was brought from there to be buried near Hazrat Mian Mir Sahib, who was her spiritual mentor. Apparently the tomb was constructed by Aurangzeb. It lies in the centre of a big tank projected by a causeway on south.

The tomb is square in plan, each side being 44 feet long. It is two-storeyed structure and measuring from the grave platform its total height comes to 32'- 6". The height of the first storey is 13 feet. The pavilion in constructed of burnt bricks with kankar lime mortar and bears recessed openings on all the four sides, three each, in both the storeys. The central openings are arched, while those on the sides are flat. Whole of the structure of the pavilion was originally lime-plastered.

The grave, which lies in the centre of the pavilion, is 10 feet 10 inches long, 2 feet 10 inches wide and 1 foot 8 inches high. There were arched small holes on the northern end of the grave on a raised portion for lighting up the area with oil lamps. On the northern face of the grave 'Bismillah' and the whole *Kalimah* are laid in marble slab in the pietra-dura design in *Nastaliq* character, while on the southern end name of the deceased and her date of demise is written on marble slab in the same design.

There are four arched openings on the ground floor in the interior around the grave and above them exactly of the same type arches are built in the upper storey. All these arched openings in both the storeys are cusped in design.

In the interior of both these storeys the ceilings and faces of the walls are decorated with traditional Mughal architectural feature of "*ghalibkari*", panels of various geometrical shapes and bear traces of red, green and black colours. The colour schemes appear to be carried over the whole of its interior surface, except the dado of the upper storey, which was brilliantly embellished with glazed tiles of multi-colours, traces of which still remain.

All the four façades of the pavilion are decorated with blind cusped arches and panels. They contain projecting, over which rises the high parapet wall.

Nadira Begum, wife of the unfortunate Prince Dara Shikoh, died of dysentery during his wandering in Sindh at the time of the war of succession to the throne between him and Aurangzeb, his younger brother

Smadh of Jhingar Shah Suthra. The northern fortification wall of the Lahore Fort, belonging to Sikh period, may also be seen behind it.

35. Name of Monument: Smadh of Jhingar Shah Suthra.

a) Owned and maintained by Government (DAP)
b) Category/Classification II
c) Character & Date/Period Hindu, Religious/
d) Whether demarcated Yes
e) Area 1K-5M-49 sft, 4K-17M-49 sft
  1K-12M-73 sft
f) Number & date of Notification: No. SRO.616(k)68,
  Dated 21.9.1968.

DESCRIPTION:

The Smadh with its other buildings, lying adjacent to the northern wall of the Fort, is the original and only site belonging to the sect of the Hindus known as Suthra (pure and true). As such it is sacred to a large number of the followers of this sect. The founder of the sect, Jhingar Shah, was a well-revered *faqir* (mendicant) in the time of Emperor Aurangzeb. It is reported that under the order of the Emperor he was allowed to collect 3 pies per shop per year in the whole of Mughal Empire.

The Smadh, which is built of brick with marble facing embellished with pietra dura and some carving. It is placed on a platform, which with an extended period of neglect, is in crumbling stage. Not only that much of the facing material, as also the doors, is gone the very fabric of the edifice is fast decaying for want of any attention.

Masti Gate.

36. Name of Monument: Masti Gate.

a) Owned and maintained by   Government (DAP)
b) Category/Classification   II
c) Character & Date/Period
d) Whether demarcated
e) Area   2K-11M, 141 Sft.
f) Number & date of Notification: S.R.O. No. 704(k)/66,
                                  Dated 26.7.1966.

DESCRIPTION:

Masti Darwaza (Gate) is a corruption of *Masjidi Darwaza,* or more appropriately *Masiti Darwaza* from the Punjabi word *Masit* for Mosque. It is thought to be called so after the neighbouring Mosque built by Maryam Zamani Begum, mother of Jahangir, in 1614 AD. The present building of the gate is of the British period.

Masti Dawaza (Gate) is a corruption of Masjidi Darwaza, or more appropriately Masiti Darwaza from the Punjabi word Masit for Mosque. It is thought to be called so after the neighbouring Mosque built by Maryam Zamani Begum, mother of Jahangir, in 1614 AD

Bhati Gate.

37.   Name of Monument: Bhati Gate.

a) Owned and maintained by   Government (DAP)
b) Category/Classification   II
c) Character & Date/Period
d) Whether demarcated
e) Area   2K-11M, 141 Sft.
f) Number & date of Notification: No. S.R.O. No. 704(k)/66,
                                    Dated 26.7.1966.

DESCRIPTION:

Bhati Darwaza (gate) is so called after the Bhattis, a Rajput tribe, a colony of whom originally was situated in this quarter. The Hindu Shahiya Kings of Kabul, who after they were driven out from Peshawar and Ohind (present Hund) by Mahmud of Ghazna in about 1008 AD made Lahore their capital. It were these people, who, according to the historian Sharif-e-Muhammad bin Mansur, were the Bhatti Rajputs. It is after these Bhattis that this gate and the locality came to be known. The present building of the gate was constructed during British period.

Sheranwala Gate, Outer.

38. Name of Monument: Sheranwala Gate.

a) Owned and maintained by   Government (DAP)
b) Category/Classification   II
c) Character & Date/Period
d) Whether demarcated
e) Area   G-7M, 142 Sft.
f) Number & date of Notification: No. S.R.O. No. 704(k)/66,
                                     Dated 26.7.1966.

DESCRIPTION:

It is said that the gate derives its name from the fact that two domesticated lions were kept here in cages by Maharaja Ranjit Singh. According to still another version, the depiction of lions on the gate earned it this name though earlier it was known as Khizri Darwaza after Khwaja Khizr, a patron saint of running waters and streams, according to common Muslim belief. This was so because in those days the gate opened to the ferry on the River Ravi, which flowed by its side.

The present building was constructed during the British period.

It is said that the gate derives its name from the fact that two domesticated lions were kept here in cages by Maharaja Ranjit Singh

Sheranwala Gate, Inner.

Kashmiri Gate.

Kashmiri Darwaza (Gate) is so called from the fact of its facing in the direction of Kashmir. The present building of the gate is of British period

39. Name of Monument: Kashmiri Gate.

a) Owned and maintained by   Government (DAP)
b) Category/Classification   II
c) Character & Date/Period
d) Whether demarcated
e) Area   G-12M, 1159 Sft.
f) Number & date of Notification: No. S.R.O. No. 704(k)/66,
Dated 26.7.1966.

DESCRIPTION:

Kashmiri Darwaza (Gate) is so called from the fact of its facing in the direction of Kashmir. The present building of the gate is of British period.

40. Name of Monument: Lahori – known as Lohari - Gate.

a) Owned and maintained by   Government (DAP)
b) Category/Classification   II
c) Character & Date/Period
d) Whether demarcated
e) Area   1K-10M-35 Sft.
f) Number & date of Notification: No. S.R.O. No. 704(k)/66, Dated 26.7.1966.

The Lohari Darwaza (Gate), a corruption of Lahori Darwaza, is the gate on the south named after the city of Lahore itself

DESCRIPTION:

The Lohari Darwaza (Gate), a corruption of Lahori Darwaza, is the gate on the south named after the city of Lahore itself. The present building is of the British period probably built according to the original plan and design. It bears an inscription in English and Urdu reading as follows: -

Sir Robert Montgomery, K.C.B., being lieutenant Governor, T.D. Frosyth Esquire, C.B. Commissioner, Captain Hall, Deputy Commissioner.

Lohari Gate.

Delhi Gate.

41. Name of Monument: Delhi Gate.

a) Owned and maintained by	Government (DAP)
b) Category/Classification	II
c) Character & Date/Period	
d) Whether demarcated	
e) Area	3K-1M-24Sft.
f) Number & date of Notification:	No. S.R.O. No. 704(k)/66,
	Dated 26.7.1966.

DESCRIPTION:

Delhi Gate (locally pronounced as Dilli Darwaza) is situated in the fortification wall towards east facing Delhi city, which earns it this name. It is one of those famous gates of city of Lahore, which is very busy for the movement of the people because of the establishment of Lahore Railway Station outside of this gate. A road leads to Lahore Fort through this old gate. The famous Wazir Khan Mosque is situated inside the gate in its vicinity. The present two storeyed structure of the gate was built during the British period and renovated during the 1980s.

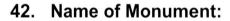
Jani Khan's Tomb.

42. Name of Monument: Jani Khan's Tomb.

a) Owned and maintained by

Owned privately, maintained by
Government (DAP)

b) Category/Classification

II

c) Character & Date/Period

Muslim, Religious/
AH1140 / 1727 AD
AH 1192 / 1778 AD

d) Whether demarcated

Yes

e) Area

67 feet x 67 feet.

f) Number & date of Notification:

No. F.4-114/58-PVT.
Dated 29.12.1959.

DESCRIPTION:

Jani Khan was the second son of Nawab Qamaruddin Khan, Wazir of Mughal Emperor Muhammad Shah (1719 - 1748 AD). Qamaruddin Khan along with his two sons, Mir Moinul Mulk and Jani Khan bravely opposed Ahmad Shah Abdali at Sirhind on 11th March 1748 AD (AH1161). In this battle Qamaruddin was killed by cannon ball while at prayers in his tent, but Abdali was defeated on account of the bravery shown by his two sons. As a result of this, the new Mughal Emperor Ahmad Shah then appointed Jani Khan as a second Bakhshi in 1748 AD and further in 1751 AD (AH 1165) he was made Wazir and entitled as Intizamud Daula Khani-e-Khanan. He was murdered by Imadul Mulk Ghaziuddin Khan on November 26, 1759, but according to Tahqiqat-e-Chisti he died in AH1192 / 1778 AD and was buried in this tomb, built by his sister, who was the wife of Nawab Zakariya Khan, in AH1140 / 1727 AD.

The Tomb, rectangular in plan (27' x 25'), is a small building with three arched openings on each side and with a beautiful curvilinear roof of a very pleasing shape decorated with enamelled mosaic work in zigzag pattern. The interior is also decorated with floral and plant decorations in fresco. There are three *katcha* graves in it, the originals might have disappeared during the Sikh period. Originally the tomb was surrounded by a garden, which has now disappeared. The remains of the gate to the south still existed when Kanhiya Lal wrote his history towards the end of 19th century.

The condition of the monument, which lies in the Ghass (grass) Mandi area on right side of the G.T.Road, near the Tomb of Mahabat Khan, has been marred by the encroachment that now stand too close to it, as also the neglect over the last many decades. It looks in an advanced stage of deterioration while, looking at the attitude of the authorities, there is no hope of its getting any share in the preservation efforts that might be underway for some more known and more important antiquity.

Jani Khan was the second son of Nawab Qamaruddin Khan, Wazir of Mughal Emperor Muhammad Shah (1719 - 1748 AD). Qamaruddin Khan along with his two sons, Mir Moinul Mulk and Jani Khan bravely opposed Ahmad Shah Abdali at Sirhind on 11th March 1748 AD (AH1161)

Glazed tiles Mosque or Zakariya Khan Mosque.

43. Name of Monument: Mosque with Glazed Tile work.

a) Owned and maintained by   Private
b) Category/Classification   I
c) Character & Date/Period   Muslim, Religious/
                                     Middle of 18th century AD
d) Whether demarcated   No
e) Area
f) Number & date of Notification: No. F.39-4/45-G,
                                     Dated 31.1.1947.

DESCRIPTION:

This is the last mosque of Mughal period, which is attributed to Nawab Zakariya Khan, the last vigorous governor of the Mughals in Punjab. After the Sikh raids at the fag end of the Mughal rule towards the middle of the 18th century, the capital of Lahore was shifted to this place and gardens and mosques were built over here. This mosque counts as one of the constructions of that period. This magnificent mosque is surmounted by one of the biggest curvilinear domes. . In front of the mosque, on east, are the ruined graves of Bahu Begum, the founder of the mosque, and some other ladies.

Till very recently the mosque stood within an open area, but now a small colony of unauthorised constructions has come up towards its east. The west and north are still open but towards south the area has been enclosed by, a sort of abandoned, Yatim Khana Darul Furqan. As it is a living mosque the local people are looking after it, though without any eye on the historic importance of the structure

The whole edifice was once decorated on the inside and the outside with enamelled tile work, either on terracotta or *'gutch'* base. However, most of this decoration now stands either obliterated or covered with lime wash as a modern maintenance approach of the unmindful Faithful looking after the edifice.

44. Name of Monument: Mosque of Nawab Zakariya Khan.

a) Owned and maintained by	Private
b) Category/Classification	I
c) Character & Date/Period	Muslim, Religious/ AH 1144 / 1731 AD
d) Whether demarcated	No
e) Area	
f) Number & date of Notification:	No. F.17-107/55 - Est, Dated 27.8.1956.

The Mosque of Nawab Zakariya Khan is situated west of tomb of Madhu Lal Hussain at Lahore. Nawab Zakariya Khan was known as Khan Bahadur of Province of Lahore. The Mosque has got three arches and on the façade of central arch Bismillah and Kalimah Sharif are written

DESCRIPTION:

The Mosque of Nawab Zakariya Khan is situated west of tomb of Madhu Lal Hussain at Lahore. Nawab Zakariya Khan was known as Khan Bahadur of Province of Lahore. The Mosque has got three arches and on the façade of central arch *Bismillah* and *Kalimah Sharif* are written. Actually the courtyard of the Mosque was paved with tiles and enclosed by a high burnt-brick wall.

On the northern arch several verses written in Persian script give some information regarding the construction of the Mosque. Date of the construction of the Mosque has also been indicated in the Persian verse as AH 1144, which corresponds to 1731 AD.

This monument being a living mosque has been saved from ruination as some other antiquity in this area. However, even though some of the decorations, inscriptions and general structure are original the building mainly stands yellow-washed and interfered with fittings to provide electric lights and fans for the *namazis* (Muslims saying their prayers). In this case as well the residential quarters have come too close to the monument.

45. Name of Monument: Hujra Mir Mehdi (Janazgah)

a) Owned and maintained by   Government (DAP)
b) Category/Classification   I
c) Character & Date/Period   Muslim, Religious/ AH 1144 (1731 AD)
d) Whether demarcated   No
e) Area
f) Number & date of Notification: No. F.17-107/55-Estt, Dated: 27.8.1956.

Hujra – cell – of Mir Mehdi in fact makes a part of the Janazgah (place for funeral prayers) and could date back to the middle of the 16th century AD and therefore, is one of the earliest existing monuments of Lahore. However, there seems to be heavy modern intervention in the structure, leaving perhaps only the shell to represent the originality

DESCRIPTION:

Hujra – cell – of Mir Mehdi in fact makes a part of the *Janazgah* (place for funeral prayers) and could date back to the middle of the 16th century AD and therefore, is one of the earliest existing monuments of Lahore. However, there seems to be heavy modern intervention in the structure, leaving perhaps only the shell to represent the originality. The monument is now surrounded on its two sides by the houses and on the rest two sides there are *katcha* approach roads.

Hujra Mir Mehdi.

Although termed as belonging to the Category I in the records, and also shown as owned and maintained by the Department of Archaeology, Pakistan, there is hardly any indication of its having been attended since long.

Sarwwala Maqbra.

46.Name of Monument: Sarvwala Maqbra

a) Owned and maintained by	Government (DAP)
b) Category/Classification	II
c) Character & Date/Period	Muslim Secular/ Middle of 18th Century AD*
d) Whether demarcated	No
e) Area	0.11 Acre (1k – 2m)
f) Number & date of Notification:	No.777 Dated: 26.8.1912

The building is the tomb of Sharfun Nisa Begum, the sister of Nawab Zakariya Khan, surnamed Khan Bahadur Khan (d.1745 AD), governor of Lahore during the reign of Mughal Emperor Muhammad Shah (1719-1748 AD). The tomb is locally known as Sarvwala Maqbara (the cypress tomb), from its ornamentation of cypress trees

DESCRIPTION:

Lying near Dai Anga's mausoleum, there is a solid, tower-like, tapering brick-built structure with *chhajja* (pent) near the top and surmounted by a four-sided pyramidal low dome carried over a double, low neck.

The building is the tomb of Sharfun Nisa Begum, the sister of Nawab Zakariya Khan, surnamed Khan Bahadur Khan (d.1745 AD), governor of Lahore during the reign of Mughal Emperor Muhammad Shah (1719-1748 AD). The tomb is locally known as Sarvwala Maqbara (the cypress tomb), from its ornamentation of cypress trees. These cypresses, four on each side, are intercepted by smaller blooming flower plants, all in enamelled tile mosaic work, on plaster base.

The square tomb carries the burial chamber at its top, at a height of about 16 feet, approachable only by stepladder. The idea of keeping the grave at such a height not easily approachable seems to have stemmed from the intention of keeping it out of sight in veneration of the pious lady.

This tomb is the last of the monuments of Mughal period. According to Latif, the tower was formerly surrounded by a beautiful garden and tank, which have now totally disappeared. Instead, a regular colony of houses has come too close to it under the aegis of the Punjab Auqaf Department, which leased out – in turn to be sold by the lessees – the land around it mainly to its employees. Most of the decoration is now gone leaving a small portion to suggest the beauty it represented in its originality.

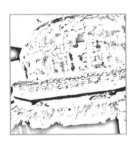

It is an impressive structure built in cut brickwork and originally decorated with beautiful tile mosaic work the traces of which still exist over the door openings

A Mughal period tomb.

47. Name of Monument: A Mughal Period Tomb

a) Owned and maintained by

Owned privately/ maintained by Government (DAP)

b) Category/Classification   II
c) Character & Date/Period
d) Whether demarcated   Yes
e) Area
f) Number & date of Notification: No. F.4.5/59-PVT.
                                       Dated 20.2.1959.

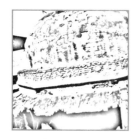

Most of the structure is fast decaying, falling bricks being the common site all over. Once situated in the open fields, the tomb is now surrounded with modern constructions

DESCRIPTION:

Situated in the fields just opposite the Police Post of Singhpura, a suburb of Baghbanpura, it is an impressive structure built in cut brickwork and originally decorated with beautiful tile mosaic work the traces of which still exist over the door openings. It is rather surprising that this tomb has not been mentioned by Latif or other authors on the subject. As there is no inscription or other evidence at the site, it is not possible to identify the personality buried here, or to exactly place it in the period it was built. However, the size of the bricks, the shape of the dome and the design and taste of tile mosaic work in which yellow colour predominates, indicate that the tomb was constructed when Shahjahani style and taste were still alive. Inside the tomb all decorations have been mutilated and disfigured. The tomb is accessible through an opening on the north. In the local dialect such an under ground chamber is called *Bhora*, hence the tomb called *Bhorewala Maqbra*.

This is another monument, which presents a sorry state of preservation. Most of the structure is fast decaying, falling bricks being the common site all over. Once situated in the open fields, the tomb is now surrounded with modern constructions. The unwieldy residential colony has encroached upon so much that there is hardly any space left to even attend or view the monument properly. The place normally remains untidy with discarded plastic shopping bags and other such material littered everywhere.

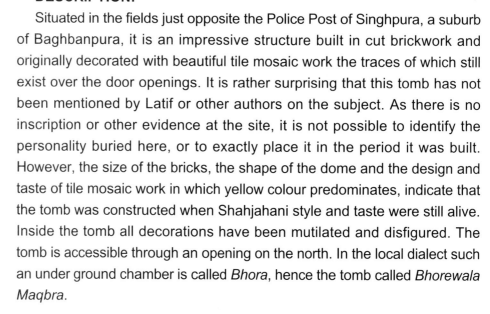

Smadh of Bhai Wasti Ram.

48. Name of Monument: Smadh of Bhai Wasti Ram.

a) Owned and maintained by	Government (DAP)
b) Category/Classification	II
c) Character & Date/Period	Sikh period/ (1799-1829 AD)
d) Whether demarcated	Yes
e) Area	1K-10M
f) Number & date of Notification:	No. F.4-81/59-Estt., Dated 26.7.1960.

DESCRIPTION:

This Smadh is situated adjacent to the northern fortification wall outside the Lahore Fort. It is entirely built in marble and represents a beautiful

specimen of architectural achievement during the Sikh period in the 19th century. It commemorates the cremation of Bhai Wasti Ram, who was the spiritual guide of Maharaja Ranjit Singh. Originally it was enclosed by a wall, which is now all but gone. It had long been occupied by the displaced persons, presumably from East Punjab, but was regained by the Department of Archaeology, Pakistan, in 1973, before the Islamic Summit Conference was held in Lahore, for some of programmes of which the Fort and the Badshahi Mosque were the important venues.

It is not in any enviable state of preservation or maintenance as it is nominally under the control of the Federal Department of Archaeology while the area, which had been turned into a garden, stands transferred to Lahore Development Authority and the Fort itself now being controlled by the Punjab Archaeology Department. Much of its marble facing has given way, thus exposing the brick core of the building, while at the same time tendering it prone to further damage – and possible obliteration – if no early restoration work were taken in hand.

Originally it was enclosed by a wall, which is now all but gone. It had long been occupied by the displaced persons, presumably from East Punjab, but was regained by the Department of Archaeology, Pakistan, in 1973, before the Islamic Summit Conference was held in Lahore, for some of programmes of which the Fort and the Badshahi Mosque were the important venues

Tomb of French officer's Daughter.

49.   Name of Monument: Tomb of French Officer's Daughter.

a) Owned and maintained by	Government (DAP)
b) Category/Classification	II
c) Character & Date/Period	Christian, Religious/ Built during Sikh Period.
d) Whether demarcated	Yes
e) Area	48K-16M-136F.
f) Number & date of Notification:	No. F.5-7/61-A&M Dated 18.10.1961.

DESCRIPTION:

The tomb stands on a mound to the east of main road from Old Anarkali to Jain Mandir, or west to the Tomb of Hazrat Mauj-e-Darya in the southwest corner of the modern building of Income Tax & Customs House. The area, however, is known as *Kuri Da Bagh* or Garden of the Girl, meaning daughter, after once presence of a garden where the daughter of French General of Maharaja Ranjit Singh lies burried.

Originally it was the site of the garden laid by General Ventura, an Italian trainer of the Sikh army. However, the place served as the residence of another European General, M. Allard, who hailed from France and was an officer in the services of Maharaja Ranjit Singh.

The daughter of General M. Allard, named Marie Charlott, died on 5th April, 1827 in Lahore and was buried on a mound in the northwest corner of this garden. General M. Allard also died due to heart attack in January 1889 during the campaign of Peshawar and his body was brought to Lahore and buried by the side of his daughter in the same tomb.

The building of this small tomb with a dome is octagonal in plan. The outer sides measure 6 feet 6 inches and inner sides measure 5 feet with two graves in the centre. The mound is also paved and edged with modern bricks. The chamber is built in country bricks with kankar lime plaster. On the top of the main entrance, a tablet with Persian script is fixed bearing the name of the builder and the date of the death of Marie Charlott, which is AH 1242/1827 AD.

The monument was not in a happy state of preservation when the present inheritors of General Allard, from St. Tropez in France, visited the place in 1980-81. They sponsored the conservation/restoration project, which was carried out by the Northern Circle of Archaeology in 1981 to make it somewhat stable structure to give it an enhanced ease of life.

Kuri Da Bagh or Garden of the Girl, meaning daughter, after once presence of a garden where the daughter of French General of Maharaja Ranjit Singh lies burried. Originally it was the site of the garden laid by General Ventura, an Italian trainer of the Sikh army. However, the place served as the residence of another European General, M. Allard, who hailed from France and was an officer in the services of Maharaja Ranjit Singh

Well of Raja Dina Nath.

50. Name of Monument: Well of Raja Dina Nath (Chowk Wazir Khan, Lahore).

a) Owned and maintained by   Government (DAP)
b) Category/Classification   II
c) Character & Date/Period
d) Whether demarcated   Yes
e) Area   336 Sft.
f) Number & date of Notification: No. S.R.O. 1616(K)68
                                  Dated 21.9.1968.

DESCRIPTION:

Raja Dina Nath was the person, who rose to remarkable power in the later days of Ranjit Singh. In 1834 Raja Dina Nath was made finance Minister. After annexation of Lahore by the British in 1849, Raja Dina Nath was appointed to the Council of Regency.

During his time the Raja constructed buildings and gardens for public welfare. Among these was the well he built opposite the white dome in the front of Masjid Wazir Khan. The well was set under a dome and open arches provided for drinking of water by the people. It was done by the Raja in 1851 AD at the suggestion of the Deputy Commissioner of Lahore. The well, though still existent and antiquity, is no more in functioning order.

The monument, along with other protected antiquity in the vicinity, is now under the charge of the Punjab Government. However, its originality is hardly recognisable with the construction of shops right against its structure.

Sikh Complex of Monuments: Smadh of Ranjit Singh, Sher Singh, Nau Nihal Singh and Shrine of Guru Arjun Mal. Note the modern gate, with its high enclosure wall, that make it inaccessible to general visitors.

51. Name of Monument:	Smadhs of Ranjit Singh, Kharak Singh and Nau Nihal Singh.
a) Owned and maintained by	Government (DAP)
b) Category/Classification	I
c) Character & Date/Period	Sikh, Religious/ 1839-48 AD
d) Whether demarcated	Yes
e) Area	
f) Number & date of Notification:	No. 1551, dated 20.9.1913.

DESCRIPTION:

Built in 1848, on the spot where Maharaja Ranjit Singh (ruled 1799-1839) was cremated almost nine years earlier, the Smadh is a beautiful mélange of Hindu, Sikh and Muslim architectural styles. A large double-storied building, it was originally built on eight pillars. However, due to wear and

Sikh Complex of Monuments: Shrine of Guru Arjun Mal as seen from the Lahore Fort.

tear, small cracks appeared in the pillars that threatened to destroy the very existence of the building. The British government, anxious to protect it, ordered to put thick iron rings around all the old pillars and to erect eight additional pillars. The entire building is now supported by sixteen pillars.

The roof of the edifice, which appears to be dome-shaped from a distance, is actually built in a square shape with a fluted dome in the centre. The dome is heavily decorated with Naga (serpent) hood designs, a rich and fitting tribute to Hindu craftsmanship. The wood panels on the ceiling are covered with stained glass work and the walls have a running floral theme. The ceilings are decorated with glass mosaic or plain glasswork, which is really skilfully done, at least in the main dome.

In the centre of the sepulchral chamber is another small dome shaped marble pavilion supported by four pillars. While the interior of the chamber is adorned with frescoes of Sikh Gurus, the pavilion itself is beautifully decorated with pietra dura work, yet another allusion to secularity. Within this pavilion, in a small marble urn shaped like a lotus, lie the ashes of the mighty Maharaja.

Even in death, the Maharaja does not lie alone. Surrounding him, in smaller knob-like urns, are the ashes of four sati queens (burned alive on the pyre with their husband) and seven slave girls. The ashes of two pigeons, burnt while flying over the pyre, also have their place in the Smadh.

There are some indications that some of the material used in the construction of this edifice originally belonged to the Mughal period buildings,

Even in death, the Maharaja does not lie alone. Surrounding him, in smaller knob-like urns, are the ashes of four sati queens (burned alive on the pyre with their husband) and seven slave girls. The ashes of two pigeons, burnt while flying over the pyre, also have their place in the Smadh

Sikh Complex of Monuments: Smadh of Ranjit Singh, along with the views of the Roshnai Gate and the Badshahi Mosque.

especially in the Fort. The large marble doorframe of the main entrance to the Smadh decorated with superb *pietra dura* work, suggests it having been removed from the Shish Mahal. Similarly, about 21 other marble doorframes at different places in the building apparently also came from some other Mughal buildings in the Fort.

Ranjit Singh is not the only ruler whose ashes lie here. Within the same complex, towards the west, are the Smadhs of his son Kharak Singh and grandson Prince Nau Nihal Singh. While these mausoleums have not been decorated with the same beautiful detail, they are still no mean contribution of the Sikhs.

Although originally owned and maintained by the Archaeological Survey of (British) India, and then inherited by the Department of Archaeology, Pakistan, it went to the control of the Evacuee Trust Board, which is now responsible for the whole complex. The ensemble, which also has the Shrine of Guru Arjan Mal – the fifth Guru of the Sikhs – is now a sort of premises not easily accessible to public. Within the site it now has arrangements for hosting innumerable Sikh *Yatrees* (pilgrims) coming from India and other countries on their religious days.

Haveli Nau Nihal Singh.

52. Name of Monument: Haveli Nau Nihal Singh, including Garden & Quarters.

a) Owned and maintained by   Government (DAP)
b) Category/Classification   I
c) Character & Date/Period   Sikh, Secular/
    c. 1840 AD
d) Whether demarcated   Yes
e) Area   2453.7 sq.yards
f) Number & date of Notification: No. F.17-112/55-Estt,
    Dated 27.8.1956.

DESCRIPTION:

This lofty Haveli is reckoned among the most magnificent buildings of the city erected during the Sikh period. It was built by Nau Nihal Singh, son

This lofty Haveli is reckoned among the most magnificent buildings of the city erected during the Sikh period. It was built by Nau Nihal Singh, son of Maharaja Kharak Singh, and used by him as his private residence

Haveli Nau Nihal Singh: Some of the Sikh Frescoes decorating the interior.

of Maharaja Kharak Singh, and used by him as his private residence. It contains numerous spacious chambers, halls and balconies. The roofs are decorated with paintings and mirrors, and are worked in gold. The walls are richly and tastefully ornamented with glasses and artificial flowers.

The Haveli is used to house the Victoria Girls High School since the 1920s. As such much of the originality of the monument stands compromised to provide additional structures to meet the accommodation requirements of different classes in different times. However, one of rooms, which is lavishly embellished with fresco paintings of the original Sikh period depicting floral designs and religious themes, is kept locked and can only be seen with special arrangements.

Baradari of Maharaja Sher Singh.

53. Name of Monument:

Baradari and Smadh of Maharaja Sher Singh.

a) Owned and maintained by   Government (DAP)

b) Category/Classification   I

c) Character & Date/Period   Sikh, Religious/
Both c. 1843 AD

d) Whether demarcated   Yes

e) Area   0.43 Acres (1K-6M)

f) Number & date of Notification: No. 11078, dated 9.4.1924.

DESCRIPTION:

The Smadh of Maharaja Sher Singh is situated west of the Summer House of Shah Bilawal. It possesses no architectural pretensions and is a simple shrine of masonry work. The reason behind this simplicity could be that after the assassination of Sher Singh there was a total absence of any effective government and the political quandary had hardly left any one to give time to art and architectural contributions. The place is historically interesting because the tragic end of Maharaja Sher Singh occurred here. East of the Smadh of Sher Singh is situated the Smadh of his wife, Randhavi.

The Baradari stands close to the place of the Smadh and is also a very simple building in burnt bricks.

Presently the Smadh is almost gone, having survived only in the remains of the old structure while the Baradari is also in dilapidated condition with much of the rear of the structure razed to ground. The remaining edifice is also in danger of collapse and gives a sad story of neglect and apathy.

The reason behind this simplicity could be that after the assassination of Sher Singh there was a total absence of any effective government and the political quandary had hardly left any one to give time to art and architectural contributions

Residence of Dr. Muhammad Iqbal, now lies within cluster of buildings.

Dr. Allama Iqbal resided in this building from 1922 to 1935 as a tenant of a Hindu landlord. After independence the building was declared evacuee property and was acquired by the Department of Archaeology, Pakistan

54. Name of Monument: Residence of Dr. Muhammad Iqbal

a) Owned and maintained by   Government (DAP)
b) Category/Classification   I
c) Character & Date/Period   Muslim
20th century AD
d) Whether demarcated   Yes
e) Area
f) Number & date of Notification: No. F.4-73/58.Estt
Dated 17.3.1950

DESCRIPTION:

In the house 34-A, at McLeod Road, Poet and Philosopher Dr. Allama Iqbal resided in this building from 1922 to 1935 as a tenant of a Hindu landlord. After independence the building was declared evacuee property and was acquired by the Department of Archaeology, Pakistan. The building consists of three large sized, two middle sized and two small sized rooms, besides a corridor on the west and two verandas, one in front and the other on the east.

As the Department could not make use of it in any befitting manner, and the pressure of the encroachers almost blocking its approach from the main road, it was later transferred to the Iqbal Academy to establish their office at the place.

Jawed Manzil.

55. Name of Monument: Javed Manzil

a) Owned and maintained by	Government (DAP)
b) Category/Classification	I
c) Character & Date/Period	Muslim, Secular/ 1935
d) Whether demarcated	Yes
e) Area	About 7 Kanals
f) Number & date of Notification:	

Keeping in view the significance of this building it was converted into a historic House Museum where the relics of the great Philosopher-Poet of the East were projected for public view

DESCRIPTION:

Since his joining B.A. classes in Government College, Lahore, Allama Muhammad Iqbal, the poet-philosopher, who dreamt of a separate homeland for the Muslims of British Indian, passed most of his life in Lahore. His first residence was inside Bhati Gate from 1900 to 1905. In 1922 he shifted to McLeod Road and stayed there till 1935. In 1934 Allama Iqbal purchased a plot of land measuring about 7 kanals situated in Mauza Garhi Shahu, Mayo Road (now renamed as Allama Iqbal Road). On completion of the house at the site at a cost of Rs.42,025 Allama Iqbal shifted from his McLeod Road residence to this house in May, 1935. A rent deed of Rs.50 p.m. was signed by him in favour of his son Javed Iqbal on 21st May, 1935 for use of the front four rooms, which remained under his use till his death. It was here that his wife Sardar Begum, mother of Javed Iqbal, died on 24th May, 1935. It was also here that Allama Iqbal passed his last three years and breathed his last on 21st April, 938 in his bedroom.

Keeping in view the significance of this building it was converted into a historic House Museum where the relics of the great Philosopher-Poet of the East were projected for public view. A temporary Museum was set up and opened to public in his centenary year 1977. The Museum displayed in a nice manner the Allama's personal belongings including his degrees and certificates, original drafts of his poetic works, letters to and from him and furniture, which remained in his use. His personal dresses and crockery and cutlery of his house also made a part of the display. The models of some of the important buildings associated with the life of the Allama were put on display during his centenary year 1977.

As the museum was set up rather hastily, the mere display of objects was found failing in depicting truly his personality, which was thought so necessary to understand such a great man and enjoy a visit to his house with a touch of feelings of his company. It was, therefore, once again designed and planned to redisplay the whole museum with due emphasis on his personality and the message he had endeavoured to convey through his works.

The new Scheme of Display comprised of two phases. In the first phase the structure of the building, composed of burnt bricks and mud-mortar, was strengthened to give it an additional lease of life. The second stage envisaged the redisplay on modern lines. A grant-in-aid from the Government of Japan was used to meet the foreign exchange component of the expenditure on display-aids. The Japanese expertise in the sophisticated display techniques was utilised to plan the exhibition on scientific lines. Its blending with Pakistani know-how having better understanding of the message of the Poet of the East helped infuse life in the otherwise dead objects and succeeded in conveying the spirit behind them. The resultant House Museum came out to be a model institution in the whole of the country and was made accessible to public on 26th October 1984, with its formal inauguration.

A temporary Museum was set up and opened to public in his centenary year 1977. The Museum displayed in a nice manner the Allama's personal belongings including his degrees and certificates, original drafts of his poetic works, letters to and from him and furniture, which remained in his use. His personal dresses and crockery and cutlery of his house also made a part of the display

Tomb of Allama Iqbal: Closer look.

56. Name of Monument:

**Tomb of
Dr. Muhammad Iqbal**

a) Owned and maintained by   Government (DAP)

b) Category/Classification   I

c) Character & Date/Period   Muslim Religious
                                    Modern (1951 AD)

d) Whether demarcated   Yes

e) Area   ---   ---- ---

f) Number & date of Notification: No.F.23-23/48-Estt.
                                    Dated 13.6.1949.

DESCRIPTION:

Allama Sir Muhammad Iqbal, the poet-philosopher of the East, was born at Sialkot on 9th November 1877 (the notification, however, erroneously gives the date as 22nd February 1873). He died in on 21st April, 1938.

His small red sandstone tomb, the work on which had started in 1940 but completed in 1951, lies in the southwest corner of Hazuri Bagh, just under the shadow of the high minaret and the towering Entrance of the Badshahi Mosque. Keeping in view of his 'falsafa-e-khudi' – philosophy of self – the Mausoleum Committee, responsible for planning and constructing the edifice, had decided against taking any help from the Government. Instead, all the expenditure was borne by the disciples and admirers of the Allama in private capacity.

With its slightly battered walls, bold moulding set in cavetto just above the plinth, a specially designed low elevation - so as not to make it out of place by impeding the view of the mosque - it has a uniqueness and originality of its own.

The doorframes are in marble and so are the screens with a monogram of the poet's name cut in their centre. The top is furnished with an eave, and the roof, though pyramidal, looks almost flat. The interior, which is panelled, is entirely finished with white marble decorated with floral and geometrical designs in relief, and is also inscribed with six couplets from Zabur-e-Ajam, one of the well-known works of the Poet.

The beautiful marble cenotaph with its platform decorated with aragonite panels of different colours and headstone of translucent marble is a gift from the Afghan Government. The front side of the headstone is inscribed with two important couplets of the celebrated Poet summing up his view against racial and colour distinction, his life-long mission.

The design of the tomb, which is a creation of the architect Nawab Zain Yar Jang Bahadur of Hyderabad, Deccan, represents an admixture of Afghan and Moorish architecture to make it standout in the ensemble of the Mughal buildings. It's landscaping and further improvement was carried out during the centenary celebrations of the Great Man in the year 1977.

Architect Nawab Zain Yar Jang Bahadur of Hyderabad, Deccan, represents an admixture of Afghan and Moorish architecture to make it standout in the ensemble of the Mughal buildings. It's landscaping and further improvement was carried out during the centenary celebrations of the Great Man in the year 1977

Tomb of Allama Iqbal. Towering Entrance to the Badshahi Mosque is also seen.

The Grave inside the Tomb of Allama Iqbal.

The beautiful marble cenotaph with its platform decorated with aragonite panels of different colours and headstone of translucent marble is a gift from the Afghan Government. The front side of the headstone is inscribed with two important couplets of the celebrated Poet summing up his view against racial and colour distinction, his life-long mission

Tomb of Allama Iqbal: View indicating the setting.

The Second Islamic Summit Conference held at Lahore from 22nd to 24th February 1974, was an important landmark not only in the history of Pakistan but also that of the entire Muslim world

Islamic Summit Minar.

57. Name of the Monument   Islamic Summit Minar

a) Owned and maintained by	Federal Government
b) Category/Classification	National Monument
c) Character & Date/Period	Secular/Modern/ later half of 1970s
d) Whether demarcated	Yes
e) Area	10 K, 13 M, 193 sft.
f) Number & date of Notification:	No.F.4-92/78-AA.II.
	Dated 19th Feb. 1983.

DESCRIPTION:

The Second Islamic Summit Conference held at Lahore from 22nd to 24th February 1974, was an important landmark not only in the history of Pakistan but also that of the entire Muslim world. It was a step forward towards fostering brotherhood amongst Muslim countries. It was desirable that a monument be built in commemoration of this historic occasion. The spot thought to be ideal for locating this monument could have been a place near the Assembly Chambers where the leaders of the participating Muslim countries had joined their heads together for the solving of the problems faced by the Muslim world. Faisal Square, opposite the Assembly Chambers was selected as the most appropriate site for the purpose. The foundation stone of the monument, which was named "Islamic Summit Minar", was laid by Mr. Zulfikar Ali Bhutto, Prime Minister of Pakistan, on 22nd February, 1975 – being the first anniversary of the Conference. The work on designing the monument was entrusted to Vedat Daloky, the renowned Turkish architect, who produced a design very beautifully balanced between modern and historic architecture. The execution of the work was entrusted to National Construction Co. (Pakistan) Limited, under the supervision of Pakistan Public Works Department (PPWD).

The monument has been built in such a way as not to obstruct the view of the historic Assembly Chambers, already declared as Special Premises by the Punjab Government. Entire usable space has been created in the basement, which comprises of four halls, each measuring 17.9 metres x 7.76 metres. The obelisk is provided with covering of white marble from Peshawar district and has the words "Allah-o-Akbar", in Arabic (English: God is the Greatest) in the recesses on all its sides in gold-leaf. There are five trapezoidal elements, finished in red sandstone in relief, on each of the four sides of the Minar. The central element on each side carries the inscription (in Arabic) "Bismillah-hir-rahma-nir rahim" (In the name of God, the Most Gracious, the Most Merciful) while each of the remaining elements has the inscription bearing the Muslim profession of the Faith – La ilaha illal-lah-o-Muhammad ar-Rasool-lal-lah – "there is no god but God. Muhammad (PBUH) is His Apostle".

The work on its building was started in July, 1975. In addition to the engineers from Pakistan and Turkey about 200 stone-artisans and 500 other trained workers remained engaged to complete the project.

The Minar, which is nearly 47.25 metres (155-foot) high, is built in RCC with beautiful white marble facing. Its designed strength can hold against severe seismic jolts while it can stand the thrust of high windstorm with a velocity of 200 miles (321.8 kilometres) per hour.

The four halls of the useable space of the basement have no door-leaves denoting the openness of the Faith that allows all and sundry to enter it. Similarly, there is only one approach to this area with a lone marble-staircase that suggests the single way (agreed by all) to achieve the ultimate goal of salvation on the Day of Judgment.

Foundation stone of "Islamic Summit Minar", was laid by Mr. Zulfikar Ali Bhutto, Prime Minister of Pakistan, on 22nd February, 1975 – being the first anniversary of the Conference. The work on designing the monument was entrusted to Vedat Daloky, the renowned Turkish architect, who produced a design very beautifully balanced between modern and historic architecture.

Tomb of Mir Niamat Khan.

58. Name of the Monument   Tomb of Mir Niamat Khan In Baghbanpura.

a) Owned and maintained by   Provincial Government
b) Category/Classification   II
c) Character & Date/Period   Muslim/Religious:
                                   Emperor Shah Jahan's period
                                   (Around mid-17th century)
d) Whether demarcated   Yes
e) Area   11 M, 75 sft.
f) Number & date of Notification: No.F.3-3/96-AA.II.
                                   Dated: November 19,1996.

DESCRIPTION:

At the back of the G'hass Mandi (Grass Market) in Baghbanpura, towards the north of the Grand Trunk Road, lies the Tomb of Mir Niamat Khan, who was a commandant of artillery in the times of Mughal Emperor Shahjahan.

The quadrangular mausoleum is surmounted by a dome, which is carried over arches and beautifully embellished with ceramic work. The arches stand on pillars of solid masonry giving it the required strength. Under the dome are three white-marble graves, the central one is the largest of them and interns within it the last remains of the Mir. Syed Latif tells in his book about the presence of a garden around it in the olden times, which belonged to Husain Ali Khan, a Syed of Bara. However, presently the Mausoleum is indiscriminately encroached upon by residential buildings almost on all its sides.

ANNEXURES III

ANNEXURE: I

Fort and Shalamar Gardens in Lahore

PAKISTAN

Lahore, Punjab

N31 35 25.0 E74 18 35.0

ref: **171**

Description multiple locations

Date of Inscription: 1981

Criteria: C (i) (ii) (iii)

Inscription on the List of World Heritage in Danger: 2000

Tanks built 375 years ago to supply water to the Garden's fountains were destroyed in June 1999 to widen the road which borders the gardens on their south side. The perimeter walls of the Garden are also deteriorating.

Brief Description

These are two masterpieces from the time of the brilliant Mughal civilization, which reached its height during the reign of the Emperor Shah Jahan. The fort contains marble palaces and mosques decorated with mosaics and gilt. The elegance of these splendid gardens, built near the city of Lahore on three terraces with lodges, waterfalls and large ornamental ponds, is unequalled.

Threats to the Site:

Tanks built 375 years ago to supply water to the Garden's fountains were destroyed in June 1999 to widen the road which borders the gardens on their south side. The perimeter walls of the Garden are also deteriorating. In view of the damage observed and the threat facing the site, the Committee decided to inscribe it on the List of World Heritage in Danger, in response to a request from the Pakistani government that the international community take action to safeguard the site.

In its letter requesting the action, the Government of Pakistan expressed its appreciation for continued assistance from the World Heritage Committee and the World Heritage Centre for the conservation and development of the Shalamar Gardens. By nominating the property on the List of World Heritage in Danger, the State Party expressed its hope to increase public awareness both nationally and internationally on the importance of preserving this Moghul exemplary site of World Heritage of value, which continues to be a living cultural heritage site.

ANNEXURE II

WAFAQI MOHTASIB (OMBUDSMAN)'S SECRETARIAT

ISLAMABAD

ORDER

Complaint No.	REG. I / 1637 /83
Name of the complainant	1. Mr. Muhammad Rafique Dogar
	2. Malik Muhammad Ashraf
Agency Complained against	1. Department of Archaeology
	2. Ministry of Culture & Tourism.

In its reply the Ministry stated that on receipt of the letter from this Secretariat the Director General had been advised by telegram to cancel the No Objection Certificate given to Malik Mohammad Ashraf

Mr. Muhammad Rafique Dogar of 119 Sutluj Block, Allama Iqbal Town, Lahore, filed a complaint which alleged, generally, that the Department of Archaeology was not paying the required attention to monuments of historical significance in Lahore and mentioned, in this connexion, a number of edifices of Moghul origin which were in danger of irremediable decay. More specifically, the complainant alleged that to add to the existing and deplorable encroachment into the surroundings of even such monuments as Jahangir's Tomb, the Department had given permission to one Malik Mohammad Ashraf of Baghbanpura to construct a residential colony which would lie adjacent to the main gateway of the mausoleum and the wall of Akbari Serai, the vast qudrangle between Jahangir's Tomb and Asaf Jah's Tomb. It was submitted by the complainant that although granting of such permission was provided for in section 22 of the Antiquities Act, 1975, whereby the Director (now Director General) of Archaeology was empowered to give approval to new constructions "within a distance 200 feet of a protected immovable antiquity", yet, in view of the historical importance and archaeological magnificence of Jahangir's Tomb and its ancillary buildings, such a permission was unwise and improper and against the accepted norms of the concerned ecology and amounted to mal-administration.

2. The comments of the Ministry of Culture, Sports & Tourism were sought. In its reply the Ministry stated that on receipt of the letter from

this Secretariat the Director General had been advised by telegram to cancel the No Objection Certificate given to Malik Mohammad Ashraf. Meantime, I detained a Director General to inspect the site in Lahore. He reported that the proposed colony was being located only 60 feet from the wall of Akbari Serai and main gateway of Jahangir's Mausoleum and, howsoever beautifully constructed, it would be a blot on the general surroundings of the Mausoleum.

3   Later, another report dated 8 January 1984 from the Ministry of Culture, Sports & Tourism stated that the NOC given to Malik Mohammad Ashraf had been withdrawn by the Director General of Archaeology who had also instructed the Director of Archaeology, Northern Circle, Lahore to ensure that the decision was implemented. Thus relief was granted in this case and the complaint bore fruit.

4   However, before that happened, Malik Mohammad Ashraf, (Complaint No.2) who had been granted the N.O.C., filed a petition before me that the D.G., Archaeology, had taken the decision after due thought and after being convinced that the residential colony planned near Jehangir's Tomb would not, in any way, affect that antiquity; rather it would add to its safety and protection. It was maintained that, in any case, the N.O.C. was lawfully issued and now neither could the D.G. withdraw it himself nor was the Federal Government empowered by law to cancel it or even ask the D.G. to cancel it.

5.   Apart from examining their written submissions I heard the parties, i.e. the Director General of Archaeology, the Director, Northern Circle, Lahore, the attorney of Complainant No.2 and also his counsel, Mr. Iqbal Ahmad Malik, Advocate. The contention of the Department was that the N.O.C. had been withdrawn before the complainant No. 2 had taken any steps in pursuance of the permission to build, while the arguments on behalf of complainant No.2 rested on the stated legal position that after D.G. had given written permission no authority, not even himself, could take it back.

6   I have carefully considered all the arguments. Section 22 of the Antiquities Act, 1975, (Act VII of 1976) reads as follows:-

"Notwithstanding anything contained in any other law fro the time being in force, no development plan or scheme or new construction on or within a distance of two hundred feet of a protected immovable antiquity shall be undertaken or executed except with the approval of the Director". (Now amended from Director to Director General),"

In view of the historical importance and archaeological magnificence of Jahangir's Tomb and its ancillary buildings, such a permission was unwise and improper and against the accepted norms of the concerned ecology and amounted to mal-administration

7. The issues involved in the two complaints and the action taken by the Agency seemed to call for consideration of the following two questions:-

(a) Did the discretion exercised by the D.G. under Section 22 of the Act, amount to mal-administration?

(b) Could the approval, earlier accorded in this case by the D.G., be withdrawn/cancelled validly?

Even a plain reading of the section abundantly demonstrates that the discretionary power enshrined therein and vested in the D.G. is to be exercised fairly and reasonably and keeping in mind the nature and archaeological importance of the immovable antiquity concerned. The whole issue has, therefore, to be seen in the context of Jahangir's Mausoleum in the close proximity of which, i.e. only 60 feet away, the proposed residential colony was to be put up for which the NOC was granted.

For us in Pakistan, inhabited mainly by Muslims, the Moghul period and everything connected with it is reminder of a glorious past. Already we have been sadly remiss in neglecting these manifestations of our proud heritage, for which no one but the Government can be blamed which has full-fledged Director General of Archaeology to look after these precious antiquities

8. Now there is not an iota of doubt in the fact that this Mausoleum, and the complex within which it is situated, is one of the most, if not the most, valuable, beautiful and internationally famous historical monuments in Pakistan. In fact it enjoys a place of distinction among the well-known Moghul monuments in the sub-continent. Enlightened countries take untold pride in showing off such monuments, which are part of their cultural tradition, and expend enormous amounts on their maintenance and up-keep. For us in Pakistan, inhabited mainly by Muslims, the Moghul period and everything connected with it is reminder of a glorious past. Already we have been sadly remiss in neglecting these manifestations of our proud heritage, for which no one but the Government can be blamed which has full-fledged Director General of Archaeology to look after these precious antiquities. In view of these facts, and in the absence of visible positive efforts to maintain, protect and even restore these monuments, any act calculated to spoil the environment of an antiquity like Jahangir's Tomb can be termed as mal-administration. It would be so termed not only as an expression of educated, cultured public opinion, but also in the light of the Antiquities Act whereby the Government accepts the responsibility and is pledged to promoting the physical and environmental conditions of these historical monument.

9. Such an act cannot be explained away by saying that it was within the D.G.'s lawful discretion. In administration the use of discretion, both under law and rules, is extensive and frequent. Many of the day-

to-day decisions which comprise administration as a whole are based on the use of discretion. But it is an accepted principle that even where permitted by law and rules, discretion has to be exercised by the use of fairness and common-sense and a judicious comprehension of the circumstances pertaining to the issue in question. I would say in fact that discretion and wisdom have to go hand in had. A decision emanating from the use of discretion cannot be taken, and must not be taken, in an off-hand or cursory manner; it must be given due thought in the light of all the connected aspects of the matter. These conditions and riders apply even more forcefully to the discretionary power vested in the D.G. of Archaeology by section 22 of the Antiquities Act, because this power has to be directly related to the antiquity near which a modern construction is proposed to be put up. Needless to say that a solitary tomb without any architectural or historical value is as much an antiquity (if it has been declared as such under the Act) as Jehangir's Mausoleum. But the construction of a building even a few feet away from this tomb would not affect its importance in any way; whereas even if a building of dire public need were to be raised close to Jehangir's Mausoleum it would constitute a travesty of all accepted cultural values and a negation of the very purpose for which the Antiquities Act was promulgated. As I see it, these considerations place a heavy responsibility on the D.G. exercising the discretion given him by section 22, because this discretion is in no way unfettered or uninhibited or such as to be dictated by whim or pleasure or subjected to the risk of individual predilection. There is no doubt in my mind, therefore, that the discretion to allow construction of a modern and decidedly unsightly residential colony, with all its human and material encumbrances, in the close proximity of Jehangir's Mausoleum was not wisely exercised and thus did constitute mal-administration.

There is no doubt in my mind, therefore, that the discretion to allow construction of a modern and decidedly unsightly residential colony, with all its human and material encumbrances, in the close proximity of Jehangir's Mausoleum was not wisely exercised and thus did constitute mal-administration

10.   To the contention that the permission was lawfully granted, I would refer to the accepted opinion of administrative law experts of world renown that whereas acts of officials contrary to law are clear examples of mal-administration, it does not follow that acts of officials which are in accordance with law cannot be examples of mal-administration. It is an unfortunate truth that in developing countries like ours more mal-administration can be ascribed to acts of omission and commission performed lawfully than otherwise.

11.   At this stage I would like to say a few words about the role of the Ombudsman in the context of the discretionary powers of the

As regards the question of validity of the cancellation of the "approval" initially accorded by the D.G. under section 22 of the Act, and the implication of such a cancellation with reference to the rights of complainant No.2, it may be explained that it is on record, and my investigation also so proves, that in response to the NOC, Complainant No. 2 did not do anything whereby any vested right could have been created in his favour

administrator. As state by me above most of the decisions taken in present-day administration, not only in Pakistan but in almost all the countries of the world, are discretionary in nature. There is a reason for that. There has been a tremendous growth of government powers in the modern state. I have seen that from the least important matter like getting vaccination for a child to an international problem like putting up a steel mill, government functionaries have a say in one form or the other. Not all this say is based on legislation or is derived from rules; discretion enters into almost every decision that an administrator takes. Therefore, the life of the common man nowadays, be he a humble labourer or an industrial tycoon, is influenced and governed by the discretionary decisions of the Government and its minions. It is for this reason that even in such a prestigious forum as the International Ombudsman Conference in 1984 the consensus was that if Ombudsmen are expected to provide administrative justice for the citizen they must have the authority to investigate discretionary decisions. Fortunately in the Establishment of the Office of the Wafaqi Mohtasib (Ombudsman) Order, 1983, the definition of "mal-administration" covers almost all the ills that can arise from the exercise of discretion, and empowers the Mohtasib to look into them. In fact of all the aspects of Government decisions those based on discretion provide the most fertile field to the Ombudsman for investigate. I appreciate that it has to be so because discretion is an indispensable tool for individualization of justice in modern times. But the aim should be how to retain the benefits of discretionary decisions without sacrificing or curtailing justice and without allowing the administrator to let extraneous interests cloud his discretionary judgement.

12.   As regards the question of validity of the cancellation of the "approval" initially accorded by the D.G. under section 22 of the Act, and the implication of such a cancellation with reference to the rights of complainant No.2, it may be explained that it is on record, and my investigation also so proves, that in response to the NOC, Complainant No. 2 did not do anything whereby any vested right could have been created in his favour. The Superior Courts have held in numerous cases that locus poenitentiae in law refers to the power of receding till a decisive step is taken. If a decisive step is taken, other consideration would arise. But if that step is yet to be taken (as happened in the instant case) I see no reason to restrict the power to modify or cancel an order provided that no allegations of mala fide or arbitrariness have been made. There are none in this case. Again, in accordance with

the findings of Superior Courts, there can hardly be any dispute with the rule that apart from the provision of Section 21 of the General Clauses Act, the power of receding till a decisive step is taken is available to the Government or the relevant authorities. In fact, the existence of such a power is necessary in the case of all authorities empowered to pass orders so as to retrace any wrong step taken by them. Nothing was claimed before me by complainant No.2 to show that he had taken any step the withdrawal of which would now result in detriment to his rights or even cause him any financial loss. The upshot of this discussion is that the Director General successfully withdrew/cancelled the said approval, earlier accorded by him and thus retrace a wrong step before any rights in consequence thereof could have been created in favour of complainant No.1.

13.   In all honesty I must place on record my decided view about the approval granted by the D.G. to Complainant No.1 to build a residential colony only 60 feet away from the wall of the Mausoleum's Akbari Serai. Had the Federal Government not advised the D.G. to cancel/withdraw the permission I would most certainly have recommended to the D.G. to do so in view of the above discussion. I could do this under Article 11(b) of the President's Order No.1 of 1983, which enables me to direct an Agency, to modify or cancel the decision, process, recommendation, act or omission; which, in my opinion amounts to mal-administration.

Specially, I would draw his attention to the Jahangir's Tomb complex which, according to the report of my Director General, who visited the site, is being badly encroached upon by unauthorized constructions

14.   Before the above findings could be announced, counsel for complainant No.2 put in an application on behalf of his client that since he wished to prosecute his case before the Government in accordance with law he would like to withdraw the complaint filed by him before me. I, accordingly, dismiss the complaint as withdrawn and not pressed. My observations in the matter will, therefore, be without prejudice to his case if he presses it at some other forum in future.

15.   Before parting with this Order, I should like to advise the Ministry of Culture, Sports & Tourism, particularly the Minister, to give serious and considered care to the general complaint about deficient upkeep of Moghul and other historical monuments. Specially, I would draw his attention to the Jahangir's Tomb complex which, according to the report of my Director General, who visited the site, is being badly encroached upon by unauthorized constructions. True the land all around the monument is owned by private persons, but I am informed that ugly structures and illegal habitations are being put up in blatant

violation of the Antiquities Act, particularly so on the rear side of the monument which is normally not visible to visitors. Moreover, it is not enough for the Government to keep such valuable monuments in a good state of repair; it is also important that their surroundings should be cleared of all structures not in keeping with architecture and spirit of such antiquities, so that when foreign visitors come to see them they should know that if we are proud of these buildings we are also culturally capable of taking care of them.

16.   Copies of this order to go to the parties.

Dated 29.12 – 1985

Sd/
(SARDAR MUHAMMAD IQBAL)
WAFAQI MOHTASIB (OMBUDSMAN)

ANNEXURE III

List of Buildings notified by Government of the Punjab under Punjab Special Premises (Preservation) ordinance, 1985:-

I. Notification No. SIII-19-7/85 Dated the 21st March, 1985.

1. Aitchison College, Lahore.
2. Residency (State Guest House).
3. Lahore High Court, Lahore.
4. Assembly Chambers, Lahore.
5. Free Masons Hall, Lahore.
6. Ferozesons Building, Shahra-e-Quaid-e-Azam, Lahore.
7. Montgomery Hall (Quaid-e-Azam library), Lahore.
8. Chamba House (GOR Estate), Lahore.
9. Civil Lines police Station, Lahore.
10. Patiala Block, King Edward College, Lahore.
11. Ewing Hall, Neela Gumbad, Lahore.
12. General Post Office, Lahore.
13. State Bank of Pakistan, Nabha Road, Lahore.
14. Taj Palace, Opp. Services Hospital, Jail Road, Lahore.
15. Anarkali Tomb (Civil Secretariat), Lahore.
16. Barkat Ali Hall, Circular Road, Lahore.
17. Punjab University (Old), Lahore.
18. Museum and National College of Arts, Lahore.
19. Town Hall, Shahrah-e-Quaid-e-Azam, Lahore.
20. Lakshami Building, McLeod Road, Lahore.
21. Tomb of Malik Ayaz (Rang Mahal), Lahore.
22. Fateh Garh Gardens near Shalimar Garden, Lahore.
23. Faqir Khana Museum (inside Bhati Gate), Lahore.
24. Haveli Dhayan Singh, Texali Gate, Lahore.
25. Kamran Baradari at Ravi, Lahore.
26. Seetla Mandir (Outside Shahalami Gate), Lahore.
27. Tomb of Qutabuddin Aibak, Lahore.
28. Bedlaw Hall, Sheesh Mahal Road, Lahore.
29. Railway Station, Lahore.
30. Government College, Lahore.
31. Islamia College, Railway Road, Lahore.
32. Islamia College, Civil Lines, Lahore.
33. Government College Hostel (New Hostel), Lower Mall, Lahore.

34. Animal Husbandry College, Lahore.
35. Central Model High School, Lower Mall, Lahore.
36. Mubarik Haveli, Bhati Gate, Lahore.
37. Haveli Nawab Sahib, Mochi Gate, Lahore.
38. Cricket Pavilion, Bagh-e-Jinnah, Lahore.
39. Kinnaird College, Jail Road, Lahore.
40. Queen Mary College, Lahore.
41. Government House, Lahore.
42. Haveli Sheikh Rukandin, Lohari Gate, Lahore.
43. Gudawara (D-Block, Model Town), Lahore.
44. Chobara Chajju Bhagat near Mayo Hospital, Lahore.
45. Dayal Singh Library, Nisbat Road, Lahore.
46. Administrative Staff College, Lahore.
47. Shahdin Building Shahrah-e-Qauid-e-Azam, Lahore.

II. Notification No. S.III-19-7/85: Dated the 9th July, 1985.

1. The Shrine of Hazrat Mian Meer Sahib (R.A.)

III. Notification No. S-III-19-7/65-Vol-I: Dated the 3rd April, 1989.

1. Badshahi Masjid, Lahore.
2. Masjid Wazir Khan.
3. Sunehri Masjid.
4. Shrine of Hazrat Abdul Mu'ali.
5. Shrine of Hazrat Shah Chiragh and attached Mosque.
6. Shrine of Hazrat Aishan Sahib.
7. Shrine of Hazrat Mauj Darya Bukhari.
8. Shrine of Mian Wadda Sahib.
9. Shrine of Hazrat Sikander Shah.
10. Masjid Saleh Mohammad Kamboh.
11. Shrine of Hazrat Data Ganj Bakhsh.
12. Shrine of Hazrat Khwaja Behari.
13. Small Mosque near the Shrine of Hazrat Behari.
14. Shrine of Hazrat Madho Lal Hussain.
15. Shrine of Hazrat Miran Hussain Janjani.
16. Platform of the grave of Mian Mir's Sister.
17. Tomb of Hazrat Sabir Shah on the west of Badshahi Mosque.
18. Tomb of Hazrat Pir Makki.
19. Mazar of Hazrat Bibi Pak Daman.
20. Shrine of Hazrat Shah Jamal.

21. Tomb of Hazrat Mullah Badakhshani and its surrounding area specially the corner Burjs.
22. Small Mosque of Wazir Khan inside Taxali Gate known as the Mosque of Indies of Wazir Khan.
23. Tombs of Nawab Abdul Samad Khan and his family.
24. Chowk Masjid Wazir Khan occupied by Khokhawalas.
25. Masjid Mai Lado.
26. Shrine of Hazrat Shah Kamal.
27. Barkat Ali Islami Hall.
28. Unchi Masjid.
29. Masjid Polian.
30. Shrine of Hazrat Syed Mahmood Hazoori.
31. Shrine and Mosque of Syed Jan Muhammad Hazoori.
32. Shrine of Hazrat Syed Maulvie Nizam-ud-Din.
33. Shrine of Hazrat Sadr-ud-Din Sadr Gahan.
34. Mosque of Khwaja Ayaz.
35. Tomb of Shah Rustam Ghazi.
36. Masjid Chinian Wali.
37. Masjid Maulvi Taj Din.
38. Tomb of Hazrat Shah Ismail.
39. Tomb of Khwaja Muhammad Saeed within an enclosure opposite Nila Gumbad.
40. Tomb of Shah Sharf lying on the north of Khwaja Muhammad Saeed's Tomb.
41. Tomb of Hazrat Shah Muhammad Ismail Gilani.
42. Tomb of Hazrat Shah Shams-ud-Din.
43. Tomb and Garden of Mian Khan s/o Said Ullah Khan,, the Prime Minister of Shahjahan.
44. The Mughal Garden of Fetehgarh.
45. Shazadi ka Maqbra near it on its north surrounded by residential houses.
46. The remaining entrance gate and Baradari of the garden of Khawaja Ayaz, who was the Governor of Lahore.
47. Mosque of Khawaja Ayaz.
48. Tomb of Nawab Khan-i-Dauran Nusrat Jang Bahadur lying whin the area of Railway Workshot.
49. Tomb of Muhammad Saleh Kamboh.
50. Masjid Moran Tawaif.
51. Shrine of Hazrat Imam Gamun.
52. Tomb of Abdul Ghani between Shalamar Garden.
53. Temple and Tank of Bherron ka Than, in Ichra.

54. Smadh of Sir Ganga Ram.
55. Smadh of Chhajju Bhagat.
56. The enclosure and Grave of Mian Natha and his Goat in the General Graveyar of Mian Mir.
57. The Grave of Mulla Hamid Gujar and his relatives.
58. Shah Chiragh Chambers.
59. Hayat House No.14, Hall Road, Lahore Property Tax No. S-50, R-14.
60. Hayat House No.14, Hall Road, Lahore Property Tax No. S-50, R-14-A.

IV. Notification No. SO.CUL(INF) 6-6/68-II   Dated the 8th July, 1991.

1. Nila Gumbad Mosque, Lahore.
2. Shrine of Hazrat Abdur Razzaq Makki.

Town Hall

Shah Chiragh Chamber

Government College

Shrine of Data Ganj Bakhsh

Masjid Mai Lado

Tomb of Hazrat Shah Chiragh

Sonehri (Golden) Masjid

Museum

Ferozesons Building *Dyal Singh Library*

Railway Station *Tomb of Mian Mir*

ANNEXURE IV

NFCH has funded fourteen projects so far. Following is the detail of funded projects:

S.No	Name of Project	Executing Agency	Year	Grant	Grant Released
1.	Acquisition of Works of John Lockwood Kipling	Mr.AtharTahir, Secretary, Transport, govt of the Punjab, Lahore	1996/ 2001 cont.	Rs.687,608	Rs.687,608
2.	Publication of Book on "Ranni Kot Fort", Sind	Mr. Badr Abro, A journalist in Karachi.	1996-96	Rs.137,000	Rs.137,000
3.	Excavation at Palai, distt. Swat	Mr. Nazir Ahmad Khan, Assistant, DOAM, Karachi	1996-97	Rs.500,000	Rs.255,299
4.	Excavation and Exploration for the protection of Bhuddhist Civilization in Haripur Valley.	Dr.F.A.Durrani, former V.C. Peshawar University.	1996/ 2001 cont.	Rs.2,023,000	Rs.2,023,000
5.	Crash Programme for the repair of Lahore Fort.	Mr. Ihsan Nadiem, former Director, NCA, DOAM*	1997	Rs.4,000.000	Rs.4,000,000
6.	Conservation of Sardar Sujhan Singh Haveli, Rawalpindi.	Dr. Shaukat Mahmood, Ex. Dean of Architecture, UET, Lahore.	1998-	Rs.1,000,000	Rs.575,000
7.	Excavation of 3 archaeological Sites at Taxila.	DG. DOAM	1998/ cont.	Rs.2,706,000	Rs.2,706,000
8.	Grant to National Archives for the purchase of a photocopier Machine.	Mr. Attique Zafar Sheikh, Ex D.G., National Archives, Isb	1999	Rs.500,000	Rs.500,000
9.	Grant to Balochistan Study Centre, University of Balochistan	Dr. A. Razzaq Sabir, Director, Balochistan Study Centre, University of Balochistan.	1999	Rs.500,000	Rs.500,000
10.	Grant for organizing an International Conference on Archaeology held in January 2000.	Ministry of Culture, CRC-an NGO for conservation of Uch and DOAM.	1999/ 2000	Rs.2,155,280	Rs.2,155,280
11.	Grant to Mohatta Palace, Karachi	Secretary Culture, govt of Sind	2000 cont.	Rs.5,000,000	Rs.5,000,000
12.	Documentation of Mural Wall of Lahore Fort.	Dr. Shaukat Mahmood, Ex Dean of Architecture, UET, Lahore.	2001 cont.	Rs2,500,000	Rs. 500,000
13.	Exploration and Survey of Buddhist Rock Carvings in Swat.	Mr. Badshah Sardar, Lecturer, AIOU.	2001 cont.	Rs.642,000	Rs.300,000
14.	Preservation of Shah Chandwali gate, Rohtas Fort.	Dr. Anisur Rahman, Secretary, HWF**	2001 cont.	Rs.4,000,000	Rs.4,000,000
			Total	Rs.26,350,888	23,339,187

**   HWF – Himalayan Wildlife Fund, An NGO.**

(**Source:** Official website of NFCH – March, 2006.)

EXPLANATIONS:

a) Abbreviations:

AH	After Hijra (Islamic Calendar)
AD	Anno Domini (Gregorian Calendar).
BC	Before Christ.
C (Lower case)	Circa
DAP	Department of Archaeology, Pakistan.
DOAM	Department of Archaeology & Museums. (Earlier mentioned as DAP).

b) Units of measurement:

F	Foot, equal to 0.3048 metres.
Sft	Square feet.
Y	Yard, equal to 0.9144 metres.
M	Marla, equal to 20.9 square metres.
K	Kanal, equal to 418.06 Square metres.
A	Acre, equal to 3,344.5 square metres.

Note: Measuring units are sometimes represented by symbols as below:

' Stands for feet.

" Denotes inches.